the **complete** *series*

Slow cooking

R&R PUBLICATIONS MARKETING PTY LTD

Published by
R&R Publications Marketing Pty Ltd
ABN 78 348 105 138
PO Box 254, Carlton North
Victoria 3054, Australia
Phone: (61 3) 9381 2199
Fax: (61 3) 9381 2689
Email: info@randrpublications.com.au
Website: www.randrpublications.com.au
Australia-wide toll-free: 1800 063 296

The Complete Slow Cooking Cookbook

Publisher: Anthony Carroll
Designer: Aisling Gallagher
Food Stylist: Briony Bennett
Food Photography: Brent Parker Jones, R&R PhotoStudio
Recipe Development: Michelle Finn, R&R Test Kitchen
Proofreading: Stephen Jones

Cover recipe *Argentinean bean and vegetable stew* on page 182

ISBN 978-1-74022-734-6

Printed February 2010
Printed in China

Contents

Introduction

In earlier years, the stockpot was perfect for corned and pickled meats, ideal for soups and casseroles and superb for stewed fruits as it happily bubbled in the hearth during those cold wintry months. However, that was the limit of its usefulness. Now that you are the owner of a new electric version, you will find that there are a great number of dishes that you had never thought could be cooked so well and with so little difficulty.

Having a slow cooker is like having a genie at home, cooking while you are away. When you arrive home, delicious food is waiting and there is no preparation mess to clean up. All of this was done the night before or earlier in the day. Having a slow cooker adds a note of serenity in the kitchen. You are free to relax for a few minutes, and there is even time for a pleasant glass of wine. You do not need to rush, dinner awaits without fear of drying out or overcooking.

Another feature of the slow cooker is that it is also a marvellous food warmer and server. It is excellent for buffets and pot luck dinner parties. The low temperature setting allows you to keep previously cooked food warm so guests can help themselves. It is ideal for heat-and-serve dishes.

Because the slow cooking concept calls for long cooking, it forces you to organise in advance. It means you get set for dinner early in the day rather than relying on something fast in the evening. You can even preform some of the necessary preparation, such as cutting up the meat, peeling the vegetables and organising all the other ingredients, the evening before.

Putting the recipe together the next morning takes only a few minutes, when all the pre-organising is done

Slow cooking, made possible by low temperature, is the key to fine flavour, juiciness and lack of shrinkage, especially with meat and poultry. Food cooked at low temperature also retains more minerals and vitamins in the food. Low temperature is below 200°C and high is around 300°C.

The wrap-around heating method makes cooking in this way possible. It eliminates all of the heat concentrating on the bottom of the cooker that will generally cause scorching and will require you to spend some time stirring when the food starts to stick.

When the cooker is turned to high, you will find that this temperature is not hot

enough to brown the meat. We believe it is best to brown meat in a frying pan or in the oven prior to placing it into the slow cooker. This will enhance the flavour of your dish. You will get an even better result if you deglaze the frying pan or roasting dish with a little stock or wine then add this to your cooker.

One drawback with slow cooking is the reduction in colour of bright coloured vegetables, especially peas and beans. A way of keeping the colour constant is to only put them into your slow cooker as a last minute inclusion.

If you try experimenting with the recipes in this book, you will find the results will astound you. Your real problem will be selecting which recipe to try next, as all of our offerings are easy to assemble with local ingredients, almost cook themselves, and offer a real taste sensation.

Our chefs and kitchen staff explored the potential of slow cooking by testing hundreds of recipes, the success ratio

was very high indeed. Our real problem was selecting which recipes to leave out of the book. After creating recipes to suit the appliance and cooking method and nursing them through the testing stages to finished product, it was hard to part with any of them. However, there is compensation in knowing that what did make the final selection is the best of its type. The best casseroles, curries, soups, desserts, meats, fish, poultry and vegetarian dishes.

You will find that in addition to all the foods you know can be cooked with success in your slow cooker, there is a great range of recipes you may not have thought of previously, such as pâtés, pastes, meatloaves, puddings, breads and cakes.

You will find that cooking times vary considerably, even when cooking a recipe a second time. Times depend so much on the tenderness and texture of the particular food being cooked.

You will find that these recipes represent the tip of the iceberg in relation to the variety that can be cooked successfully in your slow cooker. Follow the basic instructions in this book and you will find that you can adapt literally hundreds of your own recipes for slow cooking.

How to clean and care for your slow cooker

- Never submerge the appliance in water. Remove the cooking bowl and place it in the dishwasher or wash with hot soapy water as soon as you empty it. Do not pour in cold water if the bowl is still hot from cooking.

- Do not use abrasive cleaning compounds. A cloth, sponge or rubber spatula will usually remove the residue – if necessary a plastic cleaning pad may be used.

- To remove water spots and other stains, use a non-abrasive cleaner or vinegar, and wipe with olive oil to restore the sparkle.

- The metal liner may be cleaned with a damp cloth or scouring pad, or sprayed lightly with all-purpose cleaner to maintain its original sheen.

- The outside of the appliance may be cleaned with a soft cloth and warm soapy water and wiped dry. Do not use abrasive cleaners on the outside.

- Care should be taken in not bumping the ceramic insert with metal spoons or water taps. A sharp knock can break or chip the bowl.

- Do not put frozen or very cold foods in the slow cooker if the appliance has been pre-heated or is hot to the touch.

Safety hints

When using electrical appliances, basic safety precautions should always be followed, including the following:

- Read all instructions and become thoroughly familiar with the unit.

- Do not touch hot surfaces – always use handles or knobs.

- To protect against electrical hazards, do not immerse cord, plugs or cooking unit in water or other liquid.

- Close supervision is necessary when appliance is in use or near children.

- Unplug from outlet when not in use, before putting on or taking off parts, and before cleaning.

- Do not operate an appliance with a damaged cord or plug or after the appliance malfunctions or has been damaged in any manner. Return appliance to nearest authorised service facility for examination, repair or adjustment.

- The use of accessory attachments not recommended by the manufacturer may cause a hazard.

- Do not use outdoors or on a wet surface.

- Do not let the cord hang over the edge of the counter or table, or touch hot surfaces.

- Do not place slow cooker units on or near a hot gas or electric burner, or in a heated oven.

- Extreme caution must be used when moving the appliance containing hot oil or other liquids.

- Always attach to appliance first, then plug cord into the wall outlet. To disconnect, turn any control to off, then remove the plug from the wall outlet.

- Do not use the appliance for other than its intended use.

pâtés and terrines

Perhaps the most unexpected of all dishes to cook in a slow cooker, pâté actually needs precisely the slow and even cooking that a slow cooker provides. Pâtés can be very simple dishes or sophisticated courses. The long, slow cooking process produces a moist rich flavour, with no dryness. Sauces, pastes and terrines also cook beautifully in the slow cooker and may be kept hot until ready to serve. If your sauces are a little too juicy, turn the slow cooker to high, remove the lid and allow the liquid to evaporate and the sauce to reduce and thicken.

Layered chicken pâté

30g/1 oz tablespoons butter
120g/4 oz chicken livers, chopped
1 white onion, finely chopped
500g/1 lb minced veal and pork combined
1 egg, lightly beaten
½ teaspoon mixed dry herbs
zest of ½ lemon
¼ cup parsley, chopped
salt and freshly ground black pepper
2 tablespoons dry sherry
½ cup fresh wholemeal breadcrumbs
250g/8 oz chicken breast fillets, finely sliced

1 Melt the butter in a frying pan and add the chicken livers, sauté until browned, then remove from pan. Add onion to pan and sauté until soft.

2 Put livers and onion in a blender or food processor and process until well blended. Combine liver mixture with all remaining ingredients except chicken meat.

3 Grease a terrine and spoon ⅓ of the mixture into its base, then cover with a layer of chicken breast slices. Spoon in a further ⅓ of meat mixture and cover with the remaining chicken breast slices. Add the remaining mixture, smooth the surface of the terrine and cover with foil or baking paper.

4 Add 5cm/2 in of water to the slow cooker and place the terrine in the cooker. Allow to cook on low for 4–5 hours or on high for 2–3 hours. Test with a skewer – if juice runs clear, the pâté is cooked.

Serves 8 • Preparation 20 minutes • Cooking 2–5 hours

Chicken liver savoury

30g/1 oz tablespoons butter
500g/1 lb chicken livers, trimmed and quartered
120g/4 oz mushrooms, sliced
1 white onion, finely chopped
¼ cup chicken stock
1 tablespoon dry white wine
2 teaspoons dry sherry
pinch of dried thyme
salt and freshly ground black pepper
1 tablespoon plain (all-purpose) flour
1 tablespoon thickened cream
2 tablespoons fresh parsley leaves

1 Heat the butter in heavy-based frying pan and sauté the livers until lightly browned. Push to one side of pan or place in slow cooker.

2 Add mushrooms and onion to pan and sauté until softened, then pour into slow cooker with liquids, thyme and salt and pepper. Cook on high for approximately 2 hours or on low for approximately 4 hours.

3 Pour off some of the liquid into a small saucepan and blend with the flour. Bring to the boil and simmer until thickened, stirring constantly, then pour back into slow cooker and reheat. To serve, stir in cream and spoon mixture onto buttered toast quarters. Garnish with parsley.

Serves 4 • Preparation 25 minutes • Cooking 2–4 hours

Farmhouse pâté

30g/1 oz butter
250g/8 oz chicken livers, cleaned and chopped
1 large white onion, finely chopped
500g/1 lb minced veal and pork combined
zest of ½ lemon, grated
1 tablespoon brandy
1 tablespoon dry white wine
½ teaspoon dried thyme
4 rashers bacon, rind removed

1 Heat the butter in a frying pan and brown the chicken livers and onion. Process the mixture in a blender or food processor and combine with all other ingredients except bacon.
2 Place 2 rashers bacon lengthwise in a small terrine. Spoon in meat mixture and press down firmly with back of spoon. Place the remaining bacon/rashers on top. Cover with aluminium foil, then terrine lid.
3 Pour a little water into the slow cooker and cook terrine on low for approximately 4–5 hours.
4 Remove, drain off any excess fat and allow to cool. Garnish with fresh herbs or a bay leaf. If desired, a little aspic may be made up and poured over and around terrine, or set in a shallow dish then roughly chopped and used to garnish terrine.

Serves 6 • Preparation 25 minutes • Cooking 4–5 hours

Jellied chicken terrine

1 large whole chicken (2kg/4 lb)
1 onion, sliced
salt and whole peppercorns
1 bouquet garni
¼ small bunch chives, finely chopped
1 tablespoon dry sherry
¼ cup parsley, chopped
400g/14 oz canned capsicum (bell pepper) pieces, drained
1 heaped tablespoon aspic or gelatine

1 Place chicken into slow cooker with onion, salt and peppercorns and bouquet garni. Add water to cover, and cook on low for 5–6 hours or on high for 3–4 hours, (check from time to time, as exact cooking time may vary).

2 Take chicken from cooker, remove the flesh from the bones and dice finely. Place meat into a large bowl and add chives, sherry, parsley and capsicum (bell pepper) pieces.

3 Strain the stock into a saucepan and boil until reduced in quantity, then take 2 cups of stock and strain again. Heat, add aspic or gelatine, stir thoroughly and adjust seasoning.

4 Add stock to chicken mixture and combine well. Pour into a greased terrine and chill until firmly set. Serve on toast.

Serves 4 • Preparation 30 minutes • Cooking 3–6 hours

Turkey pâté

1kg/2 lb frozen turkey hindquarter
3 chicken stock cubes, crumbled
1 onion, sliced
1 stalk celery with leaves, sliced
1 carrot, roughly diced
salt and freshly ground black pepper
2 tablespoons chopped liverwurst sausage
1 teaspoon dried thyme
4 spring onions, finely chopped
¼ cup parsley, chopped
½ cup thin cream
2 tablespoons coleslaw dressing

1 Thaw turkey hindquarter and remove as much fat and skin as possible, then place into slow cooker with stock cubes, onion, celery, carrot and salt and pepper to taste.

2 Cook on low for approximately 5–6 hours or on high for 4–5 hours. Test for tenderness. When cooked, remove turkey, carefully wipe off any residual fat and allow to cool. Remove as much turkey meat as possible from the bones, then dice.

3 Using a food processor or blender, combine diced turkey meat, liverwurst, thyme, onions, parsley and a little of the cream.

4 Combine remaining cream with dressing and pour in, blending until quite smooth. Add salt and pepper to taste. Serve in small pots, accompanied by very lightly buttered wholemeal bread.

Serves 6–8 • Preparation 30 minutes • Cooking 4–6 hours

Country pâté

30g/1 oz butter
250g/8 oz calf's liver, chopped
250g/8 oz lean bacon, chopped
2 medium onions, chopped
2 tablespoons brandy
1 heaped teaspoon salt
1 teaspoon peppercorns
1 teaspoon dried thyme
¼ teaspoon aspic or gelatine
¼ cup beef stock
¼ cup parsley, chopped
sour cucumber pickles

1 Heat the butter in a frying pan and lightly brown the liver pieces, bacon and onion.
   Add brandy, salt, peppercorns and thyme and process mixture very roughly in a food
   processor or blender.

2 Lightly butter a terrine, spoon in the mixture and level off the top. Cover with
   aluminium foil. Pour a little water into the slow cooker and cook terrine on low for
   approximately 4 hours or on high for about 3 hours.

3 Dissolve the aspic or gelatine in water according to packet directions, then place in a
   small bowl, add stock and parsley and mix. Allow to stand until beginning to thicken,
   then spoon over top of terrine. Chill well. Garnish with sliced sour cucumber pickles.

Serves 6 • Preparation 25 minutes • Cooking 3–4 hours

Potted terrine

1½kg/3 lb shin of beef, sliced
2–3 fresh pig's trotters
salt and freshly ground black pepper
1 teaspoon peppercorns
2 teaspoons white vinegar
1 carrot
1 sprig thyme
1 stalk celery, sliced
3 whole sprigs parsley, plus ¼ cup chopped
2 large ham steaks (approximately 500g/1 lb total), cubed
½ cup peas, cooked and drained
1 spring onion, finely chopped
2 teaspoons gelatine

1 Place beef slices, trotters, salt, peppercorns, vinegar, whole carrot, thyme, celery and whole parsley sprigs in slow cooker. Cover with 3 cups cold water. Cook on low for approximately 8 hours or overnight.

2 Carefully remove meat and carrot from cooker and set aside. Slice the carrot. Strain stock through muslin or a fine sieve (if you want a fine stock, do this twice). Reserve 1–1½ cups of stock and keep any remainder for soups.

3 Carefully trim fat and gristle from beef slices and finely chop the meat. Remove any meat from the trotters and chop finely. Place meats in a bowl and add chopped parsley, ham cubes, peas, carrot and spring onion.

4 Dissolve the gelatine in a little hot water and stir into reserved stock, then pour over meat mixture and stir gently. Adjust seasoning if necessary, spoon mixture into a loaf tin or terrine and chill. Serve sliced with a green salad.

Serves 6–8 • Preparation 30 minutes • Cooking 8 hours

soups

You can extend the pleasures of the winter soup pot to all months of the year. A light, clear soup provides a delicious prelude to a more substantial meal, regardless of the season. Often summer-jaded palates appreciate the delicacy of a consommé or chilled soup and the slow cooker provides these without hours of slaving over a hot stove. For those hearty soups, try starting your soup on a Friday night and gently cooking it through the night to serve when the team arrives for Saturday lunch.

Consommé

1kg/2 lb lean beef on the bone, such as gravy beef
1 leek, roughly chopped
1 large onion, roughly chopped
2 bay leaves
1 clove garlic, chopped
1 stalk celery with leaves, roughly chopped
3 whole sprigs of parsley, plus ¼ cup, chopped
salt and freshly ground black pepper
¼ cup dry sherry

1 Place all ingredients except parsley and sherry in slow cooker and add 12 cups of
   water. Simmer on low for 8 hours or longer. Allow to stand until cold.
2 Carefully remove all the fat and take out all large pieces of meat and vegetables,
   then strain the consommé through gauze or a fine nylon sieve. Serve piping hot with
   2 teaspoons of dry sherry in each bowl and a sprinkle of freshly chopped parsley to
   garnish.

Serves 6 • Preparation 20 minutes • Cooking 8 hours

Dinner party beef consommé

60g/2 oz butter
1 white onion, finely sliced
400g/14 oz canned beef consommé
1 small carrot, julienned
½ stalk celery, sliced thinly on the diagonal
½ small parsnip, julienned
salt and seasoned pepper blend
2 teaspoons brandy
¼ cup parsley or chives, chopped

1 In a frying pan, melt the butter and sauté the onion until soft.
2 Add onion to slow cooker with 1 cup water and all remaining ingredients except
   brandy and parsley or chives. Simmer for 8 hours on low, ready for serving at dinner.
3 Add brandy and serve garnished with parsley or chives.

Serves 2–3 • Preparation 20 minutes • Cooking 8 hours

Lamb shank broth

2 lamb shanks
salt and freshly ground black pepper
1 carrot, diced
1 parsnip, diced
2 stalks celery, sliced
½ turnip, diced
1 white onion, diced
½ cup barley
60g/2 oz chopped parsley, plus extra to garnish

1 Place lamb shanks in slow cooker and cover with water almost to the top of the cooker. Add salt and pepper and simmer overnight on low. Allow to cool, then skim off the fat.
2 Remove the shanks, which should be very tender, and chop the meat. Return meat to stock with all other ingredients and simmer for at least 8 hours on low (or much longer if desired). Serve very hot, sprinkled with a little extra fresh parsley.

Serves 6 • Preparation 20 minutes • Cooking 16 hours

Chicken and oat soup

1½kg/3 lb chicken
2 chicken stock cubes
2 carrots, diced
1 parsnip, diced
2 onions, diced
2 stalks celery, sliced
120g/4 oz rolled oats (coarse oatmeal)
¼ cup commercial soup mix
salt and freshly ground black pepper
¼ cup parsley, chopped

1 Place the chicken in the slow cooker, cover with water and add crumbled stock cubes. Cook on low overnight. The next day, remove the chicken from the stock and allow stock to cool. Skim off fat.

2 Remove breast meat from the chicken, chop finely and put aside. The remainder of chicken meat may be used in sandwiches, chicken croquettes, chicken loaf, and so on.

3 Add all remaining ingredients to the stock in the slow cooker. Simmer on low for at least 8 hours or overnight, adding the chicken breast meat during the last hour. Adjust seasoning if necessary, and serve with a sprinkling of extra parsley in each bowl.

Serves 10 • Preparation 30 minutes • Cooking 16 hours

Minestrone

1 veal shank, trimmed of fat
1 clove garlic, crushed
1 carrot medium, finely chopped
1 large onion, chopped
2 cups beef stock
1 teaspoon salt
1 teaspoon freshly ground black pepper
3 cups tomato juice
3 tomatoes, chopped
2 teaspoons Vegemite or yeast extract
2 bay leaves
1 sprig thyme
½ cup parsley, chopped
½ cup macaroni
60g/2 oz cabbage, shredded

1 Combine all ingredients in the slow cooker. Simmer for at least 10 hours on low.
2 Remove shank from soup once meat is falling from bone, and chop coarsely. Replace meat in slow cooker and cook on high until thoroughly reheated. Taste the soup, and if the tomatoes have made it 'sharp', add a little raw sugar. Garnish with Parmesan cheese and serve with crusty bread.

Serves 6–8 • Preparation 25 minutes • Cooking 10 hours

Creamy pumpkin soup

500g/1 lb bright yellow pumpkin, peeled and cut into chunks
2 cups tomato juice
1 tablespoon raw sugar
2 chicken stock cubes, crumbled
dash of Tabasco
1 bay leaf
salt and freshly ground black pepper
½ cup thickened (pouring) cream
¼ cup parsley, chopped

1 Combine all ingredients except cream and parsley in slow cooker with 8 cups of water. Cook until pumpkin is tender, approximately 4–5 hours on low or 3 hours on high.

2 Remove bay leaf and process the mixture, a cupful at a time, in a blender or food processor. Return mixture to slow cooker and reheat. About 1 hour before serving, add cream and allow to heat through. Serve sprinkled with fresh parsley.

Serves 6–8 • Preparation 25 minutes • Cooking 3–6 hours

Tomato, lentil and basil soup

½ cup brown lentils
1kg/2 lb Roma tomatoes
2 onions, diced
2 tablespoons sun-dried tomato purée
3 cups vegetable stock
1 bay leaf
freshly ground black pepper
½ cup fresh basil, chopped

1 Rinse the lentils, drain and add them to a large saucepan of boiling water. Simmer, covered, for 25 minutes or until tender, then drain, rinse and set aside.

2 Meanwhile, place the tomatoes in a bowl, cover with boiling water and leave for 30 seconds, then drain. Remove the skins, deseed and chop.

3 In a slow cooker on high, add the onions and stir in the tomatoes, tomato purée, stock, bay leaf and pepper. Cover and simmer for 2¼ hours.

4 Remove and discard the bay leaf, then purée the soup until smooth in a food processor or with a hand-held blender. Stir in the lentils and chopped basil, then reheat on high. Serve garnished with the fresh basil leaves.

Serves 4 • Preparation 40 minutes • Cooking 3 hours

Roasted tomato, capsicum and bread soup

2 tablespoons olive oil
1kg/2 lb Roma tomatoes
2 red capsicums (bell peppers)
3 cloves garlic, crushed
2 onions, finely diced
2 teaspoons ground cumin
1 teaspoon ground coriander
4 cups chicken stock
2 slices white bread, crusts removed and torn into pieces
1 tablespoon balsamic vinegar
salt and freshly ground black pepper

1 Preheat oven to 180°C/350°F. Lightly oil a baking dish, place tomatoes and capsicums (bell peppers) in the dish and bake for 20 minutes or until the skins have blistered. Add in the garlic, onion, cumin and coriander for the last 5 minutes. Set aside to cool, then take out the tomatoes and capsicums (bell peppers), remove their skins and roughly chop.

2 Set slow cooker on high, add the cooked vegetables and stock and cook for 2 hours. Add bread, balsamic vinegar and salt and pepper, and cook for a further 50 minutes.

Serves 4 • Preparation 30 minutes • Cooking 2 hours 30 minutes

Pea and ham soup

1½ cups yellow or green dried peas
1 onion, diced
2 bay leaves
1 sprig thyme
salt and freshly ground black pepper
1 medium smoked ham hock
8 cups chicken or vegetable stock

1 Rinse peas and place in slow cooker. Add all remaining ingredients to slow cooker and cook on low for at least 8 hours. This soup improves with long, slow cooking, so 10–12 hours will enhance the flavour.
2 Remove bay leaves, thyme and ham hock. Cut the fat off the hock, chop the meat and replace it in the soup. Serve very hot.

Serves 6–8 • Preparation 20 minutes • Cooking 8–12 hours

Porcini soup

15g dried porcini
2 tablespoons olive oil
2 cloves garlic, crushed
1 leek, sliced
6 French shallots, chopped
300g/10 oz white mushrooms,
thinly sliced
500g/1 lb forest mushrooms such as
shiitake, oyster and Swiss brown, thinly
sliced

2 tablespoons plain (all-purpose) flour
4 cups chicken, beef or vegetable stock
1 cup thickened cream
½ bunch fresh flat-leaf parsley, chopped
30 fresh basil leaves, shredded
1 tablespoon fresh oregano
salt and freshly ground black pepper
ground nutmeg

1 Add the dried porcini to ½ cup boiling water. When the mushrooms have softened, remove them from the liquid and set aside. Strain the mushroom liquid through a muslin-lined sieve to remove any sand and grit, and reserve the liquid.

2 Heat the olive oil in a large saucepan and add the garlic, leek and shallots and cook until golden (about 3 minutes). Add all the fresh mushrooms and cook over a very high heat until they soften and their liquid evaporates (about 7 minutes). Reserve a few mushroom pieces for the garnish.

3 Transfer the leek and mushroom mixture to a slow cooker preheated on high, then sprinkle with the flour and stir well to enable the flour to be absorbed. Add the stock and the porcini, together with the reserved liquid. Stir to combine and cook for 2 hours.

4 Add the cream, then turn cooker to low and cook for a further 30 minutes or until slightly thickened. Add half the parsley and the basil and oregano and season to taste with salt and pepper. Serve sprinkled with remaining parsley, reserved mushrooms, some nutmeg and a small dollop of extra cream if desired.

Serves 6 • Preparation 40 minutes • Cooking 3 hours

Scallop chowder

12 scallops, diced
½ cup white wine
1 sprig thyme
1 bay leaf
1 cup thickened cream
12 cups milk
2 cups chicken stock
salt and freshly ground black pepper
6 green onions, chopped

1   Place scallops into slow cooker with white wine and herbs and cook on low for 1 hour.
2   Combine remaining ingredients and add to slow cooker. Cook on high for 1–1½ hours or on low for 1½–2 hours until heated through, but do not overcook.

Serves 4–6 • Preparation 10 minutes • Cooking 2–3 hours

beef

Those of us who are fully aware of the advantages of a slow cooker find life and entertaining very much simpler. With your slow cooker, preparations for the main course may be commenced the night before, and the chosen ingredients refrigerated overnight. On the morning of your dinner party, the main course—be it casserole, topside roast, braised rabbit, curry or fish—may be popped into the slow cooker, where it will practically cook itself while you enjoy the company of your guests.

Basic beef casserole

1 tablespoon vegetable oil
1kg/2 lb blade steak, trimmed and cubed
2 onions, chopped
2 beef stock cubes, crumbled
2 carrots, sliced
1 parsnip, sliced
salt and freshly ground black pepper
1 bouquet garni
30g/1 oz butter
2 tablespoons plain (all-purpose) flour

1 Heat the oil in a frying pan. Pat steak cubes dry with absorbent paper and brown
   them on all sides.
2 Add onion to pan and sauté until softened. Mix stock cubes in 1 cup hot water.
3 Place stock, meat, onion, carrots, parsnip, salt and pepper and bouquet garni in
   slow cooker. Cook for approximately 7–8 hours on low or 6–7 hours on high. Remove
   bouquet garni. Blend butter and flour together thoroughly and stir into hot casserole
   a dab at a time to thicken. Serve with rice and garnish with chopped parsley.

Serves 4–5 • Preparation 25 minutes • Cooking 6–8 hours

Beef, tomato and zucchini casserole

500g/1 lb blade steak, trimmed and cubed
2 white onions, thinly sliced
425g/15 oz canned Roma tomatoes
1 beef stock cube, crumbled
½ clove garlic, crushed
½ teaspoon dried marjoram
¼ cup parsley, chopped
salt and freshly ground black pepper
250g/8 oz zucchini, sliced

1 Place beef and onion in slow cooker. Add the tomatoes, reserving ¼ cup juice, mix the stock cube into the juice, then add to cooker with the garlic, marjoram and half the parsley. Season to taste.
2 Cook on low for 6–8 hours or on high 4–5 hours. About 1 hour before serving, add the zucchini and stir through half the remaining parsley. Serve sprinkled with the last of the parsley.

Serves 4 • Preparation 30 minutes • Cooking 4–8 hours

Beef stew with chickpeas

2 tablespoons oil
1kg/2 lb lean stewing beef, trimmed and cubed
2 onions, sliced
2 cloves garlic, chopped
1 eggplant, diced
1 cup beef stock
400g/14 oz canned whole peeled tomatoes, chopped
¼ cup tapioca
1 teaspoon ground cinnamon
1 bay leaf
2 teaspoons salt
freshly ground black pepper
400g/14 oz canned chickpeas (garbanzo beans), rinsed and drained

1 Heat the oil in a large frying pan over a medium heat. Add meat and cook for
  5 minutes, turning occasionally. Add the onions and garlic and cook for a further
  5 minutes, stirring constantly. Drain off any excess fats. Place the beef mixture and
  eggplant in slow cooker.
2 Combine stock with juice from canned tomatoes, tapioca, cinnamon, bay leaf, salt and
  pepper and pour into slow cooker, stirring well. Cover and cook on low for 8 hours.
3 Approximately 30 minutes before serving, turn to high. Stir in chickpeas (garbanzo
  beans) and tomatoes and cook for the remaining time. Serve garnished with oregano
  leaves.

Serves 6 • Preparation 30 minutes • Cooking 8 hours

Beef casserole with orange and cider

3 tablespoons vegetable oil
1kg/2 lb beef blade steak, trimmed and cubed
1 large brown onion, sliced
1 clove garlic, crushed
½ cup dry cider
2 beef stock cubes, crumbled
2 sprigs fresh thyme
2 large oranges, thickly sliced
salt and freshly ground black pepper
1 stalk celery, chopped

1　Heat oil in a frying pan and brown meat well. Add onion and garlic and sauté until golden.
2　Place mixture in slow cooker. Add cider, stock cubes, thyme, oranges, salt and pepper to taste and celery. Cook on low for 6–8 hours or high for 4–5 hours and serve.

Serves 6 • Preparation 20 minutes • Cooking 4–8 hours

Simple casserole

400g/14 oz stewing beef, trimmed and cut into 25mm/1 in cubes
1 packet French onion soup
1 bay leaf
1 sprig thyme
1 teaspoon seasoned pepper blend
1 tablespoon plain (all-purpose) flour

1 Place meat into slow cooker with 2 cups water and all remaining ingredients except the flour. Stir lightly and cook on low for at least 10 hours, until meat is tender.
2 Strain off ½ cup of the liquid into a small saucepan and blend very carefully with flour. Bring to a gentle boil, whisking constantly until thickened, then pour back into the slow cooker and stir gently. Reheat on high. Serve casserole sprinkled with parsley.

Serves 6 • Preparation 15 minutes • Cooking 10 hours

Creamy veal curry

1 tablespoon vegetable oil
500g/1 lb stewing veal, cubed and trimmed
1 large white onion, sliced
½ clove garlic, crushed or chopped
1 teaspoon curry powder
1 large red capsicum (bell pepper), sliced
2 bay leaves
¾ cup chicken or veal stock
½ cup fresh coconut milk or ¼ cup canned coconut cream

1 Heat the oil in a large frying pan and brown the veal. Add onion and garlic and sauté, then add the curry powder and cook gently for a few minutes, stirring occasionally.

2 Transfer veal mixture to slow cooker and add capsicum (bell pepper), bay leaves and stock. Cook on low for approximately 6 hours.

3 About half an hour before serving, stir in coconut milk or cream. Remove bay leaves and serve with cooked rice, garnished with coriander (cilantro) or parsley.

Serves 4 • Preparation 30 minutes • Cooking 6 hours

Fruity beef curry

500g/1 lb beef, cubed
1 large cooking apple, peeled and diced
120g/4oz dried apricots, chopped
¼ cup sultanas (golden raisins) or currants
1 strip orange zest
salt and freshly ground black pepper
1cm/½ in piece ginger, grated
1 tablespoon lemon juice
½ clove garlic, crushed
1 cup beef stock
1–2 tablespoons curry powder
2 tablespoons natural yoghurt

1 Place beef in slow cooker with apple, apricots, sultanas (golden raisins) or currants, orange zest, salt and pepper to taste, ginger, lemon juice and garlic.

2 Blend stock with curry powder, add to cooker and stir gently. Cook on low for approximately 6–8 hours or on high for 5–6 hours (time will vary depending on the meat). About 30 minutes before serving, stir in yoghurt and heat through. Serve with rice and chutney.

If preferred, beef may be browned first in a frying pan in a little oil. This improves the flavour and colour of the dish, but is not essential.

Serves 4 • Preparation 30 minutes • Cooking 5–8 hours

Gingered-up beef

3 onions, finely chopped
1 clove garlic, crushed
4cm/1½ in piece ginger, finely chopped
2 teaspoons salt
½ teaspoon Tabasco
1½kg/3 lb blade or oyster blade steak, cubed
500g/1 lb canned tomatoes, drained and chopped
1 cup beef stock

1 Place onion, garlic, ginger, salt and Tabasco in a food processor or blender and blend to a purée.
2 Mix meat and purée and allow to stand for at least 3 hours, turning meat occasionally.
3 Place meat in slow cooker and add tomatoes and beef stock. Cook on high for 1 hour, then on low for 4 hours or until meat is tender. Serve with rice, garnished with lemon quarters.

Serves 6 • Preparation 3 hours 25 minutes • Cooking 5 hours

Beef pot roast

1kg/2 lb piece beef topside
salt and freshly ground black pepper
½ cup soft wholemeal breadcrumbs
1 tomato, chopped, plus 6 peeled and sliced
2 canned anchovies, mashed
½ clove garlic, crushed
¼ cup parsley, chopped
1 teaspoon dried basil
2 small red capsicums (bell peppers), chopped
1 small onion, chopped, plus 2 sliced
1 tablespoon olive oil
plain flour

1 Wipe meat with absorbent paper and cut a deep pocket in the side. Season inside.

2 In a bowl, mix breadcrumbs, chopped tomato, anchovies, garlic, parsley, half the basil, half the capsicum (bell pepper) and the chopped onion. Season to taste. Stuff mixture into pocket of beef, pressing down firmly, and sew opening together with coarse thread.

3 Heat oil in a frying pan and brown meat on both sides, then place into slow cooker. Arrange sliced tomatoes and onions and remaining basil and capsicum (bell pepper) on and around meat. Cook on high for about 4 hours or on low for 6–7 hours.

4 To serve, remove meat from liquid and keep warm, then whisk just enough flour into gravy to thicken it. Slice meat and serve with gravy.

Serves 4–6 • Preparation 25 minutes • Cooking 4–7 hours

Corned silverside

2kg/4 lb piece silverside
zest of 1 orange
1 large sprig thyme
2 bay leaves
1 tablespoon Angostura bitters
12 black peppercorns

1 Place meat into slow cooker, cover with water and add orange zest, thyme, bay leaves, bitters and peppercorns.
2 Cook on low for at least 8 hours. If to be served cold, allow meat to cool in the liquid to keep it succulent.

Serves 8 • Preparation 10 minutes • Cooking 8 hours

Boeuf à la gardiane

2 tablespoons vegetable oil
1kg/2 lb gravy beef, cubed
1 tablespoon brandy
1 cup red wine
salt and freshly ground black pepper
1 bouquet garni
½ clove garlic, crushed
rind of ½ orange
120g/4 oz small black olives
8 sprigs fresh thyme, leaves removed and stalks discarded

1 In a heavy-based frying pan, heat the oil and brown meat.
2 In a small saucepan, heat the brandy and set it alight. Pour over meat in frying pan and allow to burn out.
3 Transfer meat and juices to the slow cooker and add red wine, salt and pepper, bouquet garni, garlic and orange rind. Cook on low for at least 5 hours or overnight.
4 Add the olives for approximately the last hour of cooking. If the sauce is too thin, remove the meat from the slow cooker, set to high and cook until reduced. Alternatively, drain off sauce and reduce it in a saucepan on the stovetop. To serve, remove the orange rind and bouquet garni and sprinkle with thyme.

Serves 6–8 • Preparation 30 minutes • Cooking 5–8 hours

Beef and red wine pot roast

2kg/4 lb piece good-quality beef, trimmed of fat
2 cloves garlic, finely sliced, plus 1 clove crushed
1 tablespoon vegetable oil
1 large onion, sliced
3 tablespoons brandy
½ cup red wine
2 fresh pig's trotters, washed and roughly chopped

3 carrots, roughly chopped
2 bay leaves
3 sprigs parsley
3 sprigs thyme
salt and freshly ground black pepper

1 Wipe beef with absorbent paper. Insert the tip of a sharp knife all over the meat and push garlic slivers into the cuts.

2 Heat the oil in a heavy saucepan and sauté the onion until soft and golden. Add the meat, turning occasionally, until well browned.

3 Warm the brandy in a small saucepan, then set alight and pour it over meat. Allow to burn out, add the wine and leave to simmer for approximately 5 minutes. Transfer meat to slow cooker.

4 Add trotters, carrots, crushed garlic and herbs to slow cooker, then pour over 1 cup warm water or milk. Season to taste and cook on low for approximately 6 hours. Test for tenderness after about 5 hours – meat must not be cooked to the point where it falls apart. Remove meat and set aside to rest.

5 Strain stock through muslin or nylon sieve and allow to stand until fat has firmed on top. Carefully skim fat off, strain the liquid again. Reduce liquid until it has thickened slightly to make a sauce. Slice beef and serve on a platter with steamed vegetables and sauce.

Serves 6–8 • Preparation 45 minutes • Cooking 6–7 hours

Braised steak

750g/1½ lb blade or topside steak, cut into four pieces
2 tablespoons plain (all-purpose) flour
60g/2 oz butter
1 brown onion, peeled and sliced
salt and freshly ground black pepper
1 cup beef stock
1 teaspoon Angostura bitters (optional)

1 Rub flour into each piece of steak on both sides.
2 Heat butter in a frying pan, add meat and brown quickly on both sides. Place meat in slow cooker. Add sliced onion to pan and sauté until golden brown.
3 Add onion to slow cooker with salt and pepper, stock and bitters, if using. Cook on low for 6–8 hours.

Serves 4–5 • Preparation 30 minutes • Cooking 6–8 hours

Paprika beef ribs

2 tablespoons plain (all-purpose) flour
1 tablespoon sweet paprika
salt and freshly ground black pepper
750g/1½ lb short beef ribs
1 tablespoon vegetable oil
3 onions, sliced
1 carrot, sliced
2 tablespoons beef stock
1 cup tomato purée
1 teaspoon sugar (optional)

1 Mix together flour, paprika, salt and pepper. Pat beef ribs dry with absorbent paper and rub with spice mixture.

2 Heat the oil in a frying pan and brown the beef ribs well. Transfer to the slow cooker.

3 Add a little more oil to frying pan, if necessary, and sauté onion until golden brown. Pour contents of pan into slow cooker, add the carrot and stock and stir.

4 Combine the purée and gently mix through meat and vegetables in slow cooker. Cook for 6–8 hours on low or 5–6 hours on high. Adjust seasoning if necessary, and if tomato mixture is a little sharp, add sugar. Allow dish to cool, remove all fat, and reheat to serve.

Serves 4 • Preparation 30 minutes • Cooking 5–8 hours

Chilli beef tacos

2 teaspoons vegetable oil
500g/1 lb minced beef
2 onions, chopped
60g/2 oz taco seasoning mix
½ teaspoon freshly ground black pepper
2 tablespoons tomato paste
½ cup beef stock
6 taco shells or corn tortillas

1 Heat the oil in a frying pan, and sauté the beef until browned. Add onion and cook until slightly softened. Stir in taco mix, pepper and tomato paste and cook for 1–2 minutes. Add stock and stir.

2 Transfer mixture to slow cooker and cook for approximately 4 hours on low. If mixture is too wet at the end of the cooking time, remove the cooker lid and cook on high until liquid has reduced.

3 Spoon beef mixture into heated taco shells or tortillas and serve at once with bowls of chopped tomatoes, cucumber and lettuce.

Serves 6 • Preparation 25 minutes • Cooking 4–5 hours

Spaghetti and meatballs

500g/1 lb minced beef
2 white onions, finely chopped
1 clove garlic, crushed
1 tablespoon vegetable oil
½ teaspoon dried basil
1 bay leaf
salt and freshly ground black pepper
400g/14 oz canned tomatoes, drained
2 teaspoons Worcestershire sauce
3 tablespoons tomato paste
500g/1 lb wholemeal spaghetti
30g/1 oz Parmesan cheese, grated

1 Mix together meat, onion and garlic, and roll into small balls. Heat the oil in a frying pan, add the meatballs and sauté until lightly browned.
2 Place meatballs into slow cooker and add all remaining ingredients, except pasta and cheese. Cook on low for approximately 4 hours.
3 Bring a large saucepan of salted water to the boil, add the spaghetti and cook for 8 minutes or until just firm in the centre (al dente). Drain, then add to slow cooker and stir through sauce. Serve sprinkled with Parmesan cheese.

Serves 4 • Preparation 25 minutes • Cooking 4 hours

Meatloaf

1 slice white bread
1 tablespoon milk
500g/1 lb minced beef
3 tablespoons natural yoghurt
30g/1 oz French onion soup mix
½ teaspoon mixed dried herbs
½ cup bran
3 spring onions, chopped
1 egg, beaten
freshly ground black pepper

1 Soak bread in milk and squeeze dry. Mix thoroughly with all remaining ingredients.
   Spoon into a greased cake tin and cover with lid or foil.
2 Place tin in slow cooker and cook on low for approximately 4 hours or on high for
   approximately 3 hours. Serve hot or cold, with a green salad.

Serves 4 • Preparation 20 minutes • Cooking 3–4 hours

Curried minced beef

1 tablespoon vegetable oil
1kg/2 lb minced beef
2 white onions, chopped
3 carrots, finely chopped
¼ cup parsley, chopped
1 tablespoon mild curry powder
1 apple, diced
½ cup beef stock
1 stalk celery, diced

1 Heat the oil in a frying pan, add the beef and onion and sauté until browned. Drain fat from the pan, then pour all ingredients into slow cooker.
2 Cook on low for 5–6 hours (test after 4 hours) or on high for approximately 3 hours. Serve curry on a bed of cooked rice.

Serves 3–4 • Preparation 20 minutes • Cooking 3–6 hours

Beef pie

2 tablespoons vegetable oil
1kg/2 lb blade or topside steak, cubed
1 onion, chopped
2 tablespoons plain (all-purpose) flour
2 beef stock cubes, crumbled
1 teaspoon Vegemite or yeast extract
1 tablespoon tomato paste
½ teaspoon salt
¼ cup parsley, chopped
1 teaspoon Worcestershire sauce
Tabasco
250g/8 oz pre-made puff pastry
2 tablespoons milk

1 Heat oil in frying pan and brown the beef and onion, then transfer to slow cooker using a slotted spoon. Add the flour to the juices in the pan, brown it, and pour in 1 cup water. Add the stock cubes, Vegemite or yeast extract, tomato paste and salt and bring to the boil, stirring.

2 Pour liquid into slow cooker with the parsley, Worcestershire sauce and Tabasco to taste, and cook on low for at least 6–8 hours or overnight. Test meat for tenderness, then spoon beef mixture into a greased pie dish and allow to cool.

3 Preheat the oven to 190°C/375°F. Slice puff pastry into long strips. Brush rim of pie dish with a little milk and fit a pastry strip around the wet rim, then use remaining strips to create a lattice across the meat. Brush lightly with milk and bake pie for 25–30 minutes.

Recipe makes one whole pie or 6 individual pies.

Serves 6 • Preparation 35 minutes • Cooking 7–9 hours

Family picnic pie

750g–1kg/1½–2 lb minced beef
1 stalk celery, sliced
2 carrots, grated
6 spring onions, chopped
1 white onion, chopped
pinch of mixed herbs
salt and freshly ground black pepper
3 tablespoons tomato sauce
¼ cup parsley, chopped
2 teaspoons Worcestershire sauce

Pastry
250g/8 oz butter, chopped
¾ cup wholemeal flour
¾ cup plain (all purpose) flour
1½ teaspoons baking powder
½ teaspoon seasoned pepper blend
1 egg, beaten

1 Combine all filling ingredients, place in slow cooker and cook on high for approximately 3 hours. If filling is too wet at the end of cooking time, stir in a little plain (all-purpose) flour and cook until thickened. Allow to cool.

2 To make the pastry, place the butter in a large mixing bowl. Add 4 tablespoons boiling water, mash butter with a fork, then stir. Add all remaining ingredients except the egg, and work mixture to a smooth dough. If necessary, add a little more flour. Allow to cool.

3 Preheat the oven to 200°C/400°F and grease a 25cm/10 in cake tin with a removable base. Set aside one-third of the pastry for the pie lid, then roughly roll out the remainder on a floured board. Press the pastry into the tin and work about 5cm/2 in up the sides. Pour filling into the pastry base.

4 Roll the pastry for the lid between two sheets of baking paper, then carefully peel off the top sheet. Invert pastry onto pie, peel off the remaining baking paper sheet and trim the edges with a sharp knife. Cut several vent holes in the pastry lid.

5 Shape the pastry trimmings into a small leaf decoration and place on top of pie, then lightly brush all over with beaten egg. Bake pie until pastry is crisp and golden, around 40–50 minutes. Best served cold.

Serves 8–10 • Preparation 60 minutes • Cooking 3–4 hours

Light vitello tonnato

750g/1½ lb fillet of veal, trimmed
1 cup white wine or dry cider
salt
10 peppercorns
1 bay leaf
1 clove garlic
1 teaspoon dried tarragon
1 large white onion, sliced
2 teaspoons white vinegar

Sauce
90g/3 oz canned tuna in water, drained
juice and zest of ½ lemon
½ cup coleslaw dressing
1 egg yolk
1 teaspoon seasoned pepper blend

1   Pour 1¼ cups water into slow cooker and veal, wine or cider, salt, peppercorns, bay leaf, garlic, tarragon, onion and vinegar. Cook on low for approximately 4 hours or on high for approximately 2½–3 hours. Check for tenderness, as times will vary depending on quality of meat – do not overcook. Allow meat to cool fully, then remove from stock and slice thinly. Reserve around 2 tablespoons of the stock.

2   To make the sauce, add the tuna, lemon juice and a tablespoon of coleslaw dressing to a food processor or blender and purée.

3   Beat the egg yolk into remaining coleslaw dressing and mix in the tuna purée, pepper blend and grated lemon zest. Add reserved veal stock and blend well – the mixture should have the consistency of thin cream.

4   To serve, arrange veal in overlapping slices on a platter, then spoon over the sauce. Serve with salad.

Serves 6 • Preparation 40 minutes • Cooking 3 hours

lamb

Slow cooking could have been invented just for the curry lovers of the world! No other method of cooking a curry seems to bring out the distinctive flavour of lamb so beautifully. The long cooking allows lamb and other ingredients to fully absorb the exotic curry flavours, and even cheaper cuts of meat may be used to produce a succulent curry every time.

Lamb boulangère

2 white onions, thinly sliced
2 potatoes, thinly sliced
2 tomatoes, peeled and sliced
salt and freshly ground black pepper
½ bunch thyme
1 clove garlic, quartered
1 small leg of lamb, trimmed of fat and gristle
½ cup beef stock

1 Layer vegetables in slow cooker, seasoning and adding thyme sprigs between layers.
2 Rub cut surfaces of garlic well over lamb, then season and place on vegetable bed.
   Pour in stock and cook on low for approximately 8–10 hours. Skim as much fat as
   possible from surface of liquid and serve lamb in thick slices, with vegetables and
   juices spooned over.

If preferred, lamb may be browned in a hot oven just before serving.

Serves 4–5 • Preparation 20 minutes • Cooking 8–10 hours

Pumped leg of lamb with Cumberland sauce

1 pumped or pickled leg of lamb, trimmed
1 large carrot, sliced
1 large onion, sliced
1 stalk celery with leaves, sliced
1 cinnamon stick
1 tablespoon raw sugar
2 teaspoons malt vinegar
1 orange, sliced
1 bouquet garni

Cumberland sauce
340g/12 oz redcurrant jam
3 tablespoons port
4 tablespoons Worcestershire sauce
3 tablespoons white vinegar
1 teaspoon brandy
grated zest of 1 orange

1 To make sauce, spoon jam into slow cooker and mash well with a fork. Add remaining sauce ingredients, stirring until smooth as possible, then place lid slightly ajar and cook on low for approximately 1 hour, stirring occasionally.

2 Place lamb in slow cooker and add carrot, onion, celery, cinnamon, sugar, vinegar, orange slices and bouquet garni.

3 Cover with cold water and cook on low for approximately 8–9 hours or overnight. Allow to cool in liquid. Slice lamb and serve cold with Cumberland sauce.

Serves 8 • Preparation 40 minutes • Cooking 8–10 hours

Boiled mutton with caper sauce

1 small leg pumped or pickled mutton
1 sprig thyme
1 bay leaf
1 sprig parsley
salt
6 peppercorns
2 large onions, sliced

Caper sauce
30g/1 oz butter
1 tablespoon plain (all-purpose) flour
½ teaspoon mustard powder
1¼ cups milk
1 spring onion, chopped
2 teaspoons salted capers, rinsed
salt and freshly ground black pepper

1 Wipe mutton with absorbent paper and place in slow cooker. Add herbs, seasoning and sliced onions, cover with cold water and cook on low for approximately 8 hours or on high for approximately 6 hours, until meat is tender. Remove meat and keep warm. Strain off and reserve ½ cup of the cooking liquid.

2 To make the sauce, melt the butter in a small saucepan, add the flour and mustard and cook for a couple of minutes, stirring constantly.

3 Mix together milk and reserved cooking liquid and gradually stir into butter and flour mixture. Whisk until smooth, then bring to the boil, reduce heat and stir for a minute or two. Add spring onion and capers and adjust seasoning. Slice the mutton and serve with caper sauce.

Serves 6–8 • Preparation 45 minutes • Cooking 6–8 hours

Lamb shanks with orange

4 lamb shanks, trimmed of fat
2 white onions, sliced
3 oranges, sliced
1 lemon, sliced
1 cup dry white wine
½ cup chicken stock
salt and freshly ground black pepper
2 bay leaves or 1 sprig rosemary
1 tablespoon Grand Marnier or Cointreau

1 Place shanks in slow cooker and arrange onions, oranges and lemon between and around shanks.
2 Mix wine and stock and season to taste. Place bay leaves or rosemary sprig on shanks and pour over wine mixture. Cook on low for approximately 8 hours or overnight.
3 To serve, remove cooked citrus slices and bay leaves and skim off as much surface fat as possible. Remove shanks carefully and place on a heated serving platter, then add liqueur to liquid, heat through on high and pour over shanks. Garnish with extra half-slices of orange and fresh herbs.

Serves 4 • Preparation 30 minutes • Cooking 8–10 hours

Lamb and eggplant casserole

1 tablespoon olive oil
1 small eggplant, sliced
250g/8 oz minced lamb
3 large ripe tomatoes, peeled and sliced
salt and freshly ground black pepper
6 fresh basil leaves, finely shredded
120g/4 oz Swiss cheese, grated

1 Heat the oil in a large frying pan over medium heat. Add eggplant and cook until golden brown. Drain on absorbent paper.
2 Add the minced lamb and cook for 3–4 minutes or until browned. Drain off any excess fat.
3 In a small casserole dish that fits into your slow cooker, arrange a layer of eggplant slices, a layer of minced lamb and a layer of sliced tomato, and sprinkle with salt and pepper and half of the basil. Cover with grated cheese. Repeat layers until casserole dish is filled, ending with a cheese layer.
4 Place casserole in slow cooker and cook on high for approximately 2 hours.

If preferred, casserole may be placed under griller (broiler) for a minute or two to brown the cheese topping before serving.

Serves 4 • Preparation 35 minutes • Cooking 2 hours

Lancashire hotpot

8 forequarter, neck or chump lamb chops, trimmed of fat
6 carrots, peeled and thinly sliced
6 parsnips, peeled and thinly sliced
6 onions, peeled and thinly sliced
6 potatoes, peeled, parboiled and sliced
salt and freshly ground black pepper
¼ cup parsley, chopped

1 Layer all ingredients except parsley in the slow cooker, ending with a layer of potatoes. Cover with water and cook on low for 8 hours or overnight, until lamb is falling off bones. Skim off any fat.

2 To serve, ladle out the meat and vegetables, spoon over the flavoursome juices and sprinkle with parsley.

This dish is wonderful with crusty bread to mop up the juices.

Serves 4–6 • Preparation 20 minutes • Cooking 8–10 hours

Greek lamb with rosemary

1½kg/3 lb lamb, trimmed and cubed
1 large white onion, finely sliced
2 teaspoons dried rosemary
¼ teaspoon freshly ground black pepper
¼ teaspoon salt
1 cup chicken or veal stock
¼ cup dry white wine
1 tablespoon plain (all-purpose) flour
3 rosemary sprigs

1　Place lamb in slow cooker with all other ingredients except rosemary sprigs.
　　Cook on low for approximately 6–8 hours or on high for approximately 5–6 hours.
2　If a thicker gravy is preferred, mix together some of the cooking liquid with plain
　　(all-purpose) flour. Either pour mixture back into slow cooker and cook on high until
　　thickened, stirring occasionally, or gently heat flour mixture on the stovetop in a small
　　saucepan, whisking until thickened, before pouring back into the slow cooker.
3　Garnish with rosemary sprigs and serve.

This dish goes nicely with a glass of chilled, pine-flavoured retsina.

Serves 6 • Preparation 25 minutes • Cooking 5–8 hours

Lamb and spinach curry

2 tablespoons vegetable oil
2 onions, chopped
2 cloves garlic, chopped
25mm/1 in piece ginger, finely chopped
1 cinnamon stick
¼ teaspoon ground cloves
3 cardamom pods
750g/1½ lb lamb, diced
1 tablespoon ground cumin
1 tablespoon ground coriander
⅓ cup natural yoghurt
2 tablespoons tomato paste
¾ cup beef stock
salt and freshly ground black pepper
120g/4 oz baby spinach, chopped
2 tablespoons blanched almonds, toasted

1 Heat the oil in a large heavy-based saucepan. Add onions, garlic, ginger, cinnamon, cloves and cardamom and cook for 5 minutes. Add the lamb and cook for 5 minutes, turning, until it begins to brown.

2 Transfer mixture to slow cooker set on high. Mix in the cumin and coriander, then add the yoghurt 1 tablespoon at a time, stirring well each time. Mix the tomato paste and stock together and add to the cooker. Season to taste, then reduce the heat to low and cook for 7 hours.

3 Stir in the spinach, cover and simmer for another 15 minutes or until the mixture has reduced slightly. Remove the cinnamon stick and the cardamom pods and mix in the almonds. Serve with rice.

Serves 4 • Preparation 40 minutes • Cooking 7–8 hours

Lamb shanks with red wine

6 lamb shanks
2 medium onions, chopped
2 cloves garlic, crushed
¼ cup plain (all-purpose) flour
¼ cup fresh coriander (cilantro), chopped
¼ cup beef stock
¾ cup red wine
2 tablespoons tomato paste
juice and zest of 1 orange
3 large sprigs fresh rosemary, leaves removed and chopped

1 Trim excess fat from the lamb shanks.
2 Place the onions and garlic in a slow cooker bowl. Put flour in a plastic bag with the lamb shanks, shake to completely coat the shanks and then place shanks in the cooker on top of the onions and garlic. Sprinkle any leftover flour over the top.
3 Combine all other ingredients in a small bowl and mix thoroughly, then spoon this over the shanks in the cooker.
4 Place lid on and cook on high for 4–5 hours or on low for 9–10 hours. Serve with green beans and mashed potatoes.

Serves 6 • Preparation 20 minutes • Cooking 4–10 hours

Slow-cooked lamb roast

1½kg/3 lb lamb roast
2 cloves garlic, cut into slivers
2 sprigs fresh rosemary
2 tablespoons olive oil
30g/1 oz butter
1 large onion, sliced
400g/14 oz canned butter beans, drained and rinsed
¼ cup flat-leaf parsley, chopped
½ cup chicken stock
salt and freshly ground black pepper

1 Make small incisions all over lamb with a very sharp knife, then stuff each with a sliver of garlic and a sprig of rosemary.
2 Heat oil in a large frying pan, cook lamb until browned all over. Remove from pan and transfer to slow cooker.
3 In the same pan, add butter and cook onion for 1–2 minutes or until transparent, then place in slow cooker with remaining ingredients except seasoning.
4 Cover and cook on high for 3–4 hours, or on low for 6–8 hours. Season with salt and pepper.
5 Remove meat from slow cooker and rest for 10 minutes before carving. Serve slices of lamb with beans and parsley sauce.

Serves 4 • Preparation 25 minutes • Cooking 3–8 hours

Easy lamb stew

1½kg/3 lb lamb shoulder, boned and cut into 25mm/1 in cubes
500g/1 lb potatoes, cut into large dice
4 large carrots, cut in 25mm/1 in pieces
1 medium onion, halved and thinly sliced
1 stalk celery, sliced diagonally
1 teaspoon salt
2 tablespoons freshly ground black pepper
1 bouquet garni
1 cup tomato purée
500g/1 lb frozen sliced green beans
250g/8 oz fresh mushrooms, cleaned and sliced
1 cup sour cream
1 tablespoon plain (all-purpose) flour

1 Put lamb into a large slow cooker. Add potatoes, carrots, onion, celery, salt, pepper, bouquet garni, tomato purée, and 2 cups water and mix. Cover and cook on low 8–10 hours.
2 Remove bouquet garni. Add green beans and mushrooms, then blend sour cream and flour, add to cooker and stir.
3 Cover and cook on high for 30–60 minutes.

Serves 8 • Preparation 30 minutes • Cooking 8–11 hours

poultry

Chicken cooked in the slow cooker is a tender and succulent treat. Because chicken flesh is tenderer than most other meats, you will need to watch it a little more carefully. The age of the chicken–often a secret between the chicken and your poulterer–makes a great difference to the length of the cooking time, so test from time to time, just to ensure that your chicken is not over-cooking. You can do this by inserting a skewer through the air-vent in the lid. As well as providing lots of rich, flavoursome stock, the chicken meat is white and tender, and not as dry as chicken cooked in the conventional way.

Drunken chicken stew

1 chicken, jointed
3 rashers bacon, rinds removed
3 white onions, thickly sliced
3 carrots, thickly sliced
¼ cup parsley, chopped
1 sprig thyme
12 peppercorns
½ clove garlic, crushed
1¼ cups white wine

1 Soak chicken in salted water for 1 hour. Drain well.
2 Cut bacon into large pieces and combine with all other ingredients in slow cooker. Cook on low for 8 hours or overnight. Remove thyme sprig and serve on a bed of cooked rice, garnished with extra parsley.

Rabbit is also delicious prepared in this way.

Serves 4 • Preparation 25 minutes • Cooking 8–10 hours

Chicken mandarin

3 white onions, sliced
1 clove garlic, crushed
2 carrots, diced
4 large chicken breast fillets
salt and seasoned pepper blend
400g/14 oz canned mandarins in syrup
1 tablespoon honey
2 teaspoons Angostura bitters
100g/3½ oz French onion soup mix
zest of ½ orange, julienned

1 Place onion, garlic and carrots in slow cooker. Coat chicken breasts evenly with mixed salt and pepper blend and place on top of vegetables.

2 Mix together the mandarin syrup, honey and bitters, then stir in the soup mix and pour into slow cooker. Cook on low for 6–8 hours. After 3 hours, add mandarin segments and orange zest.

3 Remove chicken when cooked. If liquid looks too thin, reduce on a high heat or thicken with 2 tablespoons cornflour (cornstarch). Serve on rice, and garnish with chopped parsley.

Serves 4 • Preparation 35 minutes • Cooking 6–8 hours

Citrus chicken

1 lemon
1½kg/3 lb roasting chicken
1 bouquet garni
3 carrots, thinly sliced
6 onions, thinly sliced
½ cup chicken stock
salt and freshly ground black pepper
pinch of nutmeg
1 tablespoon toasted flaked almonds
¼ cup parsley, chopped

Cream sauce
½ cup thin cream
170g/6oz button mushrooms, sliced

1 Halve the lemon, squeeze out the juice and brush it all over the chicken. Place lemon skins in the chicken cavity.

2 Lightly grease the slow cooker and add the bouquet garni. Place the chicken on top and arrange the carrot and onion around the outside. Pour around the stock, season to taste, add nutmeg, then cook for approximately 6 hours on low or 4–5 hours on high (cooking time will vary depending on the tenderness of the chicken).

3 To make the sauce, saute the mushrooms. Remove about ½ cup of chicken stock from the slow cooker, skim off as much fat as possible, and bring to the boil in a small saucepan. Add the stock and reduce, then add the cream and reduce to make a pouring sauce. Serve chicken with the cream sauce.

Serves 4–5 • Preparation 40 minutes • Cooking 4–6 hours

Mustard chicken

3 carrots, peeled and diced
3 large onions, finely chopped
1 clove garlic, crushed
2 teaspoons dried thyme
1 bay leaf
salt and seasoned pepper blend
500g/1 lb lean pork, skinned and sliced
1½kg/3 lb chicken, jointed
4 rashers bacon, rinds removed
½ cup dry white wine
¼ cup brandy

Mustard sauce
1 egg yolk
3 tablespoons thickened cream
1 tablespoon Dijon mustard

1 In a bowl, combine the carrot, onion, garlic, herbs and salt and pepper. Place half the pork in the base of the slow cooker, then add half the vegetables. Add the chicken pieces, the remaining vegetables, then the remaining pork. Place bacon rashers on top.

2 Pour over combined wine and brandy. Place a piece of foil over the slow cooker, then cover with lid and cook on low for around 5 hours (cooking time may vary depending on the tenderness of the chicken).

3 To make the sauce, drain off the cooking liquid, skim off any fat and pour into a small saucepan. Beat egg yolk and cream together, add to saucepan and whisk. Cook gently until thick, but do not allow to boil. Add the mustard and whisk until thoroughly blended.

4 Arrange chicken pieces, pork and vegetables on warmed serving platter, and pour over the mustard sauce. Serve with potatoes, sprinkled with parsley.

Rabbit can be used in this recipe instead of chicken.

Serves 3–4 • Preparation 40 minutes • Cooking 5–6 hours

Fricasséed chicken with vinegar

¼ cup olive oil
1kg/2 lb chicken thigh fillets, quartered
freshly ground black pepper
2 large cloves garlic, chopped
2 sprigs fresh rosemary, leaves removed and chopped
5 anchovy fillets, chopped
½ cup white wine vinegar
2 tablespoons balsamic vinegar
20 Kalamata olives

1 In a heavy-based frying pan, heat the olive oil and brown the chicken pieces all over, seasoning well with pepper. Transfer to a plate and keep warm. Turn the heat to low and add garlic, rosemary and anchovies. Stir until the mixture is aromatic.

2 Transfer the garlic mixture and chicken to the slow cooker. Add the white wine vinegar and cook on high for about 1½ hours or until the chicken is tender. Just before serving, stir in the balsamic vinegar and olives.

This dish is delicious served with spinach and potatoes roasted in olive oil and rosemary.

Serves 4 • Preparation 30 minutes • Cooking 1½–2 hours

Nice'n'easy Chinese chicken

1 tablespoon vegetable oil
4 chicken pieces
2 chicken stock cubes, crumbled
1 tablespoon cornflour (cornstarch)
2–3 tablespoons soy sauce
freshly ground black pepper
750g/1½lb chopped Chinese vegetables (such as bok choy, choi sum and gai lan)
3 spring onions, sliced diagonally

1 Heat the oil in a frying pan. Remove the skin from the chicken pieces, add to the pan and brown lightly.

2 Transfer chicken to slow cooker and add the stock cubes and ½ cup water. Cook on low for 3–4 hours or on high for approximately 2½–3½ hours (cooking time will vary depending on the tenderness of the chicken).

3 Blend the cornflour (cornstarch) with 1 tablespoon water and pour back into slow cooker, stirring thoroughly. Add soy sauce and pepper.

4 Turn the slow cooker to high, add the Chinese vegetables and cook for approximately 30 minutes. Add spring onions about 15 minutes before the end. Serve with cooked rice or noodles, sprinkled with chopped coriander (cilantro).

Serves 4 • Preparation 30 minutes • Cooking 2½–4 hours

Easy chicken curry

1½ kg/3 lb chicken, jointed
60g/2 oz leek and potato soup mix
1 tablespoon curry powder
zest of ½ lemon, grated
250g/8 oz green beans, blanched
salt and freshly ground black pepper

1 Trim chicken pieces and place in slow cooker. Combine soup mix and curry powder and sprinkle over and around chicken pieces. Pour over enough water to barely cover chicken and cook on high for approximately 4 hours or on low for approximately 6 hours.

2 About 1 hour before serving, stir in lemon zest and beans. Add salt and pepper to taste. Serve with cooked rice.

Serves 4–5 • Preparation 25 minutes • Cooking 4–6 hours

Green chicken curry with lemongrass rice

2 cups coconut milk
1 cup chicken stock
2 tablespoons green curry paste
3 kaffir lime leaves, shredded
200g/7 oz pumpkin, chopped
4 chicken breast fillets, cubed
120g/4 oz canned bamboo shoots, drained
120g/4 oz snake beans, chopped
200g/7 oz choysum, chopped
1 tablespoon fish sauce
1 tablespoon grated palm sugar
¼ cup fresh Thai basil leaves, torn

Lemongrass rice
1½ cups jasmine rice
2 stalks lemongrass, bruised

1 Combine coconut milk, stock, curry paste and lime leaves in a slow cooker on high. Cook until the sauce begins to thicken. Add the pumpkin and cook for 20 minutes or until it starts to soften.

2 Add the chicken and bamboo shoots and cook for 1 hour. Add the beans, broccoli, fish sauce and palm sugar and cook until the vegetables are tender, approximately 1 more hour. Stir through the basil leaves.

3 To make the lemongrass rice, put the rice, lemongrass and 4 cups water in a saucepan. Bring to the boil and cook over a high heat until steam holes appear in the top of the rice. Reduce the heat to low, cover and cook for 10 minutes or until all the liquid is absorbed and the rice is tender. Remove the lemongrass. Serve curry spooned over bowls of rice.

Serves 6 • Preparation 35 minutes • Cooking 3–4 hours

Ginger chicken and pineapple salad

1½kg/3 lb roasting chicken
salt and peppercorns
2 cloves garlic
2 small white onions, sliced into rings
30g/1 oz ginger, grated
1 pineapple, cubed
1 red capsicum (bell pepper)
2 tablespoons vinaigrette or coleslaw dressing
¼ cup parsley, chopped

1 Place the chicken in the slow cooker and cover with cold water. Add the salt, peppercorns, garlic and half the onion and ginger and cook on low for approximately 5 hours or on high for 3 hours (cooking time will vary depending on the tenderness of the chicken – the flesh should not be falling off the bones). Remove chicken from stock and allow to cool. Retain stock for soups.

2 Shred chicken into bite-size pieces. Combine with remaining onion and ginger and all other ingredients except dressing and parsley. Toss salad with dressing and garnish with parsley.

Serves 6 • Preparation 35 minutes • Cooking 3–5 hours

Chicken tropicana

1½kg/3 lb roasting chicken
1 onion, chopped
1 carrot, chopped
1 stalk celery, chopped
salt and peppercorns
30g/1 oz butter
1 tablespoon plain (all-purpose) flour
1 tablespoon curry powder
1 cup milk
juice and zest of ½ lemon
3 tablespoons thin cream
2 large mango, diced

1 Place chicken in slow cooker with onion, carrot, celery, salt and peppercorns, and cover with water. Cook on low for approximately 8 hours or overnight.

2 Remove chicken and chop coarsely, discarding skin and bones. Retain stock for soups.

3 Melt the butter in a frying pan over low heat, then add the flour and curry powder and stir for 1–2 minutes. Add the milk and bring to the boil, stirring constantly, then reduce heat and simmer until thickened, stirring constantly. Season to taste, add lemon juice and zest and stir in cream.

4 Fold chicken and mango into sauce and pour back into slow cooker on high heat and allow to heat through. Serve with rice garnished with coriander (cilantro).

Serves 4 • Preparation 40 minutes • Cooking 8–10 hours

Moroccan-style chicken wings

2 tablespoons vegetable oil
1kg/2 lb chicken wings
1 large onion, finely chopped
1 clove garlic, crushed
2cm/¾ in piece ginger, grated
½ teaspoon ground turmeric
½ teaspoon ground cumin
1 cinnamon stick
¼ cup cider vinegar
2 cups apricot nectar
salt and freshly ground black pepper
90g/3 oz pitted prunes, pitted
90g/3 oz dried apricots
1 tablespoon honey
¼ cup lemon juice

1   Heat the oil in a large saucepan and brown the chicken wings in batches. Remove browned wings to a plate. Add the onion to the pan and cook for 2 minutes. Stir in the garlic and cook for a further minute.

2   Transfer the onion and garlic to the slow cooker. Add the chicken, ginger and spices, and stir to coat wings with spices. Add the vinegar and apricot nectar, season to taste and cook on low for 6 hours.

3   Add the prunes, apricots, honey and lemon juice to the cooker and simmer for 2 more hours. Remove lid, turn to high and simmer for 35 minutes. If a thicker sauce is desired, remove the wings and fruit to a serving platter and simmer until the sauce reduces and thickens. Serve wings immediately on a bed of steamed couscous and pour over the sauce. Garnish with parsley.

Serves 6 • Preparation 40 minutes • Cooking 9 hours

Curried chicken wings

250g/8 oz potatoes, peeled
750g/1½ lb chicken wings
1 tablespoon plain (all-purpose) flour
1 tablespoon curry powder
1 tablespoon vegetable oil
1 white onion, chopped
1 cup chicken stock
salt and freshly ground black pepper
250g/8 oz carrots, peeled and sliced diagonally
6 spring onions, chopped (optional)

1 Parboil potatoes, cube roughly and set aside.
2 Wipe the chicken wings with absorbent paper and roll in the combined flour and curry powder. Heat the oil in a frying pan, brown the chicken, then place it in slow cooker set on low.
3 Add onion to frying pan and cook until softened, then add to slow cooker. Add the stock to the frying pan, stirring constantly until it boils and thickens. Season to taste and pour into slow cooker.
4 Add potatoes and carrots to cooker and cook for approximately 4 hours, testing after that time. Do not allow to overcook, as meat will fall from bones. Stir in spring onions, if using, just before serving. Serve curry with pappadums.

If carrots are rather old and woody, it is a good idea to lightly cook them before adding to slow cooker.

Serves 4 • Preparation 35 minutes • Cooking 4–5 hours

Chicken and mushroom vol-au-vents

1½kg/3lb roasting chicken
2 chicken stock cubes, crumbled
salt and freshly ground black pepper
1 bouquet garni
3 white onions, sliced
30g/1 oz butter
2–3 tablespoons plain (all-purpose) flour
1¼ cups milk
2 tablespoons dry sherry
2 tablespoons Dijon mustard
1 red capsicum (bell pepper), finely chopped
340g/12 oz canned mushrooms, drained
4 spring onions, chopped
4 medium-size vol-au-vent cases
¼ cup parsley, chopped

1 Place chicken, stock cubes, salt and pepper, bouquet garni and onions in slow
   cooker. Cover with cold water and cook on low for approximately 4–6 hours or on
   high for 3–4 hours.

2 When chicken is cooked, allow to cool and cut flesh into small cubes. Strain stock,
   reserve 1¼ cups for the sauce and retain the rest for soups.

3 Heat the butter in a saucepan over low heat, add 1 tablespoon of flour and stir for a
   minute or two. Combine milk and reserved chicken stock and gradually stir into flour
   and butter mixture, whisking constantly. Bring to the boil, then reduce heat and add
   sherry and mustard. Stir until thickened. Gently fold in cubed chicken, capsicum (bell
   pepper), mushrooms and spring onions.

4 Pour sauce mixture into the empty slow cooker and keep hot on high. Meanwhile,
   bake vol-au-vent cases in the oven according to packet directions. To serve, spoon
   chicken mixture into pastry cases and garnish with chopped parsley.

Serves 4 • Preparation 40 minutes • Cooking 3–6 hours

Chicken crêpes

1½kg/3 lb roasting chicken
2 chicken stock cubes, crumbled
1 onion, chopped
3 sprigs parsley
1 sprig thyme
120g/4 oz butter
1 spring onion, finely chopped
600g/21 oz button mushrooms, sliced
4 tablespoons plain (all-purpose) flour
salt and freshly ground black pepper
1½ cups milk
1 tablespoon dry sherry

2 tablespoons thickened cream
3 hard-boiled eggs, chopped

Crêpe batter
2 cups plain (all-purpose) flour
pinch of salt
2 eggs, beaten
1 tablespoon olive oil
2 cups milk

1 Place chicken in slow cooker, add stock cubes, onion and herbs and cover with water. Cook on low for 4–5 hours or high for 3–4 hours. Remove chicken and chop flesh finely, discarding skin and bones. Reserve ½ cup stock. Melt butter in frying pan and sauté spring onions and mushrooms until softened but not brown. Blend in flour, season and cook for 1 minute.

2 Combine the milk and reserved stock and add to the pan gradually, stirring. Add sherry and cream, then cook gently until stock thickens. Adjust seasoning if necessary and fold through cooked chicken and hard-boiled eggs. Keep mixture warm in slow cooker on high, with lid slightly ajar.

3 To make batter, sift the flour and salt together and make a well in the centre. Add the eggs, oil, and one cup of milk. Beat gradually drawing in flour from the sides. Slowly add remaining milk and 4 tablespoons water, making a thin batter. Cover and set aside for at least an hour. Heat a little butter in a heavy-based 15cm/6 in frying pan. Add a little batter and tilt pan so that batter spreads evenly. When cooked on one side, turn and cook other side. Pile crêpes in a tea towel and keep warm.

4 Preheat the oven to 180°C/360°F. Place a spoonful of chicken sauce onto each crêpe, roll up and place into a greased ovenproof dish. Spoon over some of the sauce and bake for about 10 minutes. Serve remainder of sauce in a small jug at the table.

Serves 6–8 (about 16 crêpes) • Preparation 50 minutes • Cooking 3–5 hours

Duck braised in brandy and port

1kg/2 lb plump duck
4 tablespoons plain (all-purpose) flour
60g/2 oz butter
2 tablespoons olive oil
2 rashers bacon, chopped
1 large onion, chopped
60g/2 oz small mushrooms, sliced
4 tablespoons brandy
4 tablespoons port
salt and freshly ground black pepper
½ teaspoon dried thyme

1 Pat duck dry with absorbent paper, and rub lightly with 2 tablespoons flour.
2 Heat butter and oil in a frying pan and brown duck on all sides. Remove and place in slow cooker.
3 Add a little extra butter to frying pan if necessary, then add bacon, onion and mushrooms. Sauté until golden brown. Pour half the brandy and half the port into the pan and simmer for 1–2 minutes. Add remaining flour and cook until very well browned.
4 Gradually add 1 cup water, stirring constantly. Season to taste, add thyme and spoon sauce over duck in slow cooker. Cook for approximately 5 hours on low. About 30 minutes before serving, stir remaining port and brandy into sauce around duck. Serve with green vegetables.

Serves 4 • Preparation 35 minutes • Cooking 5–6 hours

fish and seafood

To most people, the methods of cooking fish are limited to frying and baking – it is not generally considered as the basis for a meal cooked in a slow cooker. In actual fact, fish, with its delicate flesh, cooks beautifully in the slow cooker and tastes superb. Tender and juicy, it also retains its shape and texture well, providing it is not overcooked. Do remember that fish will not take as long to cook as other foods, so lift the lid from time to time towards the end of the cooking period and check the tenderness of the flesh.

Citrus and tarragon fish

600g/21 oz white fish fillets
salt and freshly ground black pepper
8 large sprigs tarragon
2 oranges, each cut into four slices
2 lemons, each cut into four slices
4 tablespoons dry white wine

1 Cut four pieces of aluminium foil and lightly butter each. Place a piece of fish on each foil sheet and season to taste.

2 Lay a tarragon sprig on each piece of fish then a slice of orange and a slice of lemon side by side. Turn up the sides of the foil and spoon 1 tablespoon wine over each fish piece, then fold over the foil and seal the parcels. Place in the slow cooker and cook on high for 1–1½ hours or on low for 2–2½ hours.

3 To serve, place parcels on serving places, open the top of each parcel and replace the cooked herb sprigs and citrus slices with fresh herb sprigs and citrus slices. Alternatively, carefully transfer the fish to the plate, replace the herbs and citrus slices, and spoon the juices over the top.

Serves 4 • Preparation 25 minutes • Cooking 1–2½ hours

Fillets Veronique

8 fillets of delicately flavoured fish
1 cup white wine
salt and freshly ground black pepper
1 bouquet garni
30g/1 oz butter
1 tablespoon cornflour (cornstarch)
½ cup thickened cream
250g/8 oz small seedless grapes

1　Place fillets in slow cooker, cover with wine and add salt, pepper and bouquet garni. Cook on low for 1–1½ hours, or until fish is tender but still firm. Drain off and reserve liquid, and discard bouquet garni.

2　Heat the butter in a frying pan, stir in the cornflour (cornstarch) and cook for a couple of minutes. Combine cream and the reserved liquid and stir well. Pour gradually into butter and flour mixture and whisk constantly until mixture boils. Cook for a minute or two, stirring all the time, until sauce thickens.

3　Pour mixture back into slow cooker and turn to high. Cook for approximately 30 minutes, add grapes and allow to heat through. Serve very hot, with sauce spooned over fillets and grapes piled on top.

Serves 4 • Preparation 30 minutes • Cooking 1½–2 hours

Smoked cod with lemon herb butter

1kg/2 lb smoked cod
a few peppercorns
½ lemon, sliced
large sprig thyme or marjoram
1 cup white wine

Lemon herb butter
120g/4 oz butter
⅓ teaspoon dried thyme
juice of ½ lemon
zest of 1 lemon, grated
¼ cup finely parsley, chopped
¼ teaspoon seasoned pepper blend

1 Cut cod into large serving pieces, removing any coarse pieces of outer skin. Place in slow cooker with remaining ingredients and add sufficient water to cover the fish.

2 Cook on low for approximately 2–2½ hours or on high for 1½–2 hours (check during cooking time to ensure that fish is not falling apart). Remove fish with a slotted spoon, arrange on a serving platter and keep warm.

3 To make the herb butter, melt butter and add all other ingredients. Spoon butter over fish to serve.

If you wish to make the butter in advance, simply beat all ingredients together (without melting the butter), then press into small pots and refrigerate.

Serves 6 • Preparation 30 minutes • Cooking 1½–2½ hours

Smoked cod casserole

1kg/2 lb cod
1 white onion, sliced
1 cup dry white wine
1 teaspoon peppercorns
1 teaspoon crushed garlic
¼ cup fennel, dill or aniseed, chopped
5 large tomatoes, plus 1 extra, quartered
10 black olives, pitted
6 spring onions, chopped into 5cm/2 in lengths

1 Cut fish into serving-size pieces and place with onion, wine, peppercorns, garlic and fennel, dill or aniseed in the slow cooker. Cook on low for approximately 2 hours. Check fish at the end of 1½ hours, as cooking time may vary depending on the tenderness of the fish and whether it has been frozen.
2 During the last 30 minutes of cooking, add four of the tomatoes and the olives. To serve, pour fish and juices into a casserole. Fold through the spring onions and garnish with remaining tomato quarters.

Serves 6–8 • Preparation 25 minutes • Cooking 2 hours

Curried scallops

250g/8 oz scallops
½ cup dry white wine
1 bouquet garni
120g/4 oz butter
1¼ cups thin cream
½ teaspoon curry powder
salt and freshly ground black pepper
2 egg yolks
2 tablespoons milk

1 Place scallops, white wine and bouquet garni in the slow cooker and cook on low for approximately 1 hour. Pour off and reserve liquid, discard bouquet garni and keep scallops warm in slow cooker.
2 Put cooking liquid with butter into a small saucepan and boil hard to reduce. Stir in the cream, curry powder and salt and pepper, and again boil hard for 2–3 minutes. Remove from heat and allow to cool.
3 Beat egg yolks with milk, and carefully stir into cooled cream mixture. Pour mixture back into slow cooker with the scallops and cook on high for 45–60 minutes. To serve, place a little cooked rice in a small bowl and spoon over 3–4 scallops with a generous quantity of sauce. Serve immediately.

Serves 6 • Preparation 25 minutes • Cooking 2 hours

Slow paella

1 tablespoon olive oil
2 onions, chopped
2 cloves garlic, crushed
4 sprigs fresh thyme, leaves removed and stalks discarded
zest of 1 lemon, finely grated
4 ripe tomatoes, chopped
2½ cups short-grain white rice
pinch of saffron threads, soaked in 2 cups water
5 cups chicken or fish stock, warmed
290g/10 oz peas
2 red capsicums (bell peppers), chopped
1kg/2 lb mussels, scrubbed and debearded
500g/1 lb firm white fish fillets, chopped
290g/10 oz raw prawns (shrimp), shelled
250g/8 oz scallops
3 calamari, cleaned and sliced
¼ cup parsley, chopped

1 Preheat slow cooker on high. Add the oil and the onion and stir, then add the garlic, thyme, lemon zest and tomatoes and cook for 15 minutes.

2 Add the rice and saffron mixture and warmed stock. Simmer, stirring occasionally, for 1½ hours or until the rice has absorbed almost all the liquid.

3 Stir in the peas, capsicums (bell peppers) and mussels and cook for 20 minutes. Add the fish, prawns (shrimp) and scallops and cook for 20 minutes. Stir in the calamari and parsley and cook for 20 minutes longer or until the seafood is cooked.

Serves 8 • Preparation 35 minutes • Cooking 60–80 minutes

Corn and tuna bake

400g/14 oz canned corn kernels, drained
¼ red capsicum (bell pepper), chopped
400g/14 oz canned tuna, drained
120g/4 oz mushrooms, chopped
1 cup thin cream
250g/8 oz Cheddar cheese, grated
¼ cup parsley, chopped
250g/8 oz wholemeal macaroni

Topping
1 cup soft wholemeal breadcrumbs
45g/1½ oz butter, melted
30g/1 oz Parmesan cheese, grated
1 teaspoon dried basil

1 Bring a large saucepan of salted water to the boil, add the macaroni and cook for
   8 minutes or until just firm in the centre (al dente). Drain, set aside and keep warm.
2 Place soup, corn, red capsicum (bell pepper), tuna, mushrooms, cream, cheese and
   parsley in slow cooker. Mix together and cook on high for 1 hour or on low for about
   2 hours, until vegetables have softened.
3 Preheat the oven to 190°C/375°F. Pour tuna mixture into a greased casserole together
   with macaroni. Mix thoroughly.
4 To make the breadcrumb topping, mix all ingredients together. Sprinkle topping over
   casserole and bake for 30 minutes or until top is golden brown.

Serves 6–8 • Preparation 35 minutes • Cooking 1½–2½ hours

vegetarian

More and more people are becoming aware of the advantages of a partly or totally vegetarian diet. Whether their reasons be economical, spiritual or philosophical, less people consider meat as an essential part of their eating pattern and are substituting soybeans, lentils, pulses, cheese and sometimes fish. Just as there are main meat courses, so there are main courses based on vegetarian ingredients. In this chapter we offer a few great ideas.

Savoury zucchini custards

30g/1 oz butter
¼ cup white onion, finely chopped
250g/8 oz zucchini, grated
salt and freshly ground black pepper
60g/2 oz Parmesan cheese, grated
60g/2 oz Cheddar cheese, grated
⅓ cup thickened cream
2 large eggs, beaten

1 Heat butter in a frying pan and sauté onions for 10–15 minutes until tender and just beginning to brown.

2 Tip zucchini into clean absorbent paper and squeeze dry. Increase the heat in the pan, add the zucchini and toss for 5 minutes or so. Cover pan and cook for several minutes longer over low heat, until zucchini is tender. Season to taste and pour into a bowl.

3 Add cheese to the bowl, pour in cream and stir well. Fold eggs into mixture, then taste and adjust seasoning if necessary. (The mixture may be refrigerated at this stage until ready to cook. If you do this, allow a longer cooking time.)

4 Grease 4 small ramekins and pour custard into each. Put dishes into slow cooker, and pour enough water into the base of the cooker to come approximately halfway up the sides of the dishes. Cook on low for 1 hour with lid ajar.

5 Cook, covered, for another 3 hours, testing for firmness at the end of that time.

Test for firmness by inserting a knife blade into one of the custards – the blade should come out clean.

Serves 4 • Preparation 40 minutes • Cooking 4 hours

Spinach custards

250g/8 oz cooked spinach or silverbeet, stems removed
120g/4 oz cream cheese
2 small eggs
½ cup milk
1 small onion, peeled and chopped
¼ teaspoon salt
freshly ground black pepper
½ teaspoon dried basil
30g/1 oz Parmesan cheese, grated
8 fresh basil sprigs

1 Drain spinach or silverbeet until as dry as possible, then process in a food processor or blender until finely chopped. Add remaining ingredients and half the basil and blend until very smooth.
2 Pour mixture into 6–8 small, buttered ovenproof dishes and cover each with aluminium foil. Place dishes in the slow cooker and pour a little water into base, then cook on high for approximately 1½ hours or on low for 2½ hours.
3 To serve, sprinkle with extra grated cheese and garnish with a basil sprig.

This dish makes a delicious light lunch served with a salad and fresh, warm bread.

Serves 6–8 • Preparation 35 minutes • Cooking 1½–2½ hours

Vegetable casserole

500g/1 lb potatoes, peeled and thickly sliced
500g/1 lb very ripe tomatoes, peeled and sliced
½ teaspoon sugar
2 white onions, thinly sliced
2 green or red capsicums (bell peppers), thinly sliced
1kg/2 lb small zucchini, sliced
salt and freshly ground black pepper
1 clove garlic, crushed
1 teaspoon dried basil
30g/1 oz butter
30g/1 oz Parmesan cheese, grated
¼ cup parsley, chopped

1 Boil the potatoes until slightly tender. Sprinkle the tomatoes with sugar.

2 Grease the base of the slow cooker and layer in the vegetables, starting with the onion. Sprinkle each layer with salt, pepper, garlic and basil. Finish with a layer of tomatoes, then dot with butter. Pour over any juice from tomato slices.

3 Cook on high for approximately 3 hours or on low for approximately 5 hours. Serve sprinkled with grated cheese and parsley.

Serves 8 • Preparation 35 minutes • Cooking 3–5 hours

Stuffed vine leaves in tomato sauce

12 grape vine leaves, canned or fresh
2 cups cooked brown rice
1 teaspoon dried mixed herbs
pinch of nutmeg
salt and freshly ground black pepper
1 teaspoon dried garlic
2 tomatoes, chopped and peeled
¼ cup parsley, chopped
½ teaspoon Angostura bitters (optional)
2 spring onions, chopped finely

Tomato sauce
15g/½ oz butter
1 onion, diced
400g/14 oz canned Roma tomatoes, drained and chopped
2 teaspoons brown sugar
pinch of dried herbs
1 tablespoon tomato paste
3 tablespoons dry red wine
¼ cup parsley, chopped

1 If you are using fresh vine leaves, remove the stems, pour boiling water over leaves and leave for 1–2 minutes until softened. Dry, and lightly wipe over each leaf with a drop of oil.

2 Combine all other ingredients to make the filling. Squeeze a handful of filling to make it firm and place onto leaf, then fold into neat little parcel, sealing with a little squeeze. Repeat with remaining leaves. Arrange carefully in base of slow cooker.

3 To make the tomato sauce, heat the butter in a frying pan and cook the onion until golden brown. Add all other ingredients and cook until blended. Spoon sauce into slow cooker over vine leaf parcels, and cook on high for approximately 1½ hours or on low for 2–2½ hours.

Serves 4 • Preparation 40 minutes • Cooking 1½–2½ hours

Pizza with slow-cooked tomato sauce

Sauce
750g/1½ lb soft ripe tomatoes, peeled
and chopped
2 tablespoons tomato paste
few dashes Angostura bitters
1 small white onion, finely chopped
salt and freshly ground black pepper
1 teaspoon sugar
¼ teaspoon dried garlic
½ teaspoon mixed herbs

Pizza dough
1 tablespoon compressed yeast
1 teaspoon white sugar
500g/1 lb plain (all-purpose) flour
pinch of salt
15g/½ oz butter
1 tablespoon vegetable oil

1   Combine all sauce ingredients in slow cooker and allow to cook on low overnight.
    If the mixture is too thin the next morning, turn cooker to high and cook, uncovered,
    until thickened and reduced. Allow to cool.

2   To make the dough, crumble the yeast into a bowl, stir in sugar and 1¼ cups
    lukewarm water until yeast has dissolved, sprinkle a little of the flour onto surface
    and set aside in a warm place until mixture froths.

3   Sift the flour and salt together and rub in butter. Pour in frothy yeast mixture and
    mix with a wooden spoon, then turn out onto a floured board and knead for at least
    5 minutes. Shape into a round and set aside in a warm place until dough has doubled
    in size.

4   Preheat the oven to 220°C/425°F. Roll dough out thinly, place on greased pizza tray or
    heated pizza stone and prick surface all over with a fork.

5   Brush pizza with vegetable oil and spread generously with tomato sauce. Add
    preferred pizza toppings (for example, cheeses, olives, basil), then place pizza in oven
    and cook for about 50 minutes.

Serves 6–8 • Preparation 50 minutes • Cooking 8–10 hours

Herbed cannelloni with tomato sauce

250g/8 oz cottage cheese
30g/1 oz Parmesan cheese, grated
1 teaspoon mixed dried herbs
6 spring onions, finely chopped
salt and freshly ground black pepper
few drops Angostura bitters (optional)
8 instant cannelloni tubes

Tomato sauce
1 cup tomato purée
3–4 spring onions, chopped
2 teaspoons Worcestershire sauce
4 drops Angostura bitters
1 large clove garlic, crushed

1 Bring a large saucepan of salted water to the boil, add the pasta tubes and cook for
   8 minutes or until just firm in the centre (al dente). Drain, set aside and keep warm.
   Place the cheeses, herbs, spring onions, salt and pepper and bitters in a bowl and mix
   thoroughly.
2 To make the sauce, mix together all ingredients.
3 Lightly butter the base of the slow cooker. Spoon cheese mixture into cannelloni
   tubes. Spoon a little tomato sauce into the cooker, then arrange the stuffed cannelloni
   tubes in the cooker and spoon over remainder of sauce. Cook for 1–1½ hours on high
   or 2–2½ hours on low. Serve sprinkled with extra Parmesan cheese and parsley sprigs.

Serves 3–4 • Preparation 25 minutes • Cooking 1½–2½ hours

Mushroom casserole

60g/2 oz butter
1kg/2 lb mushrooms, sliced
10 spring onions, chopped into 25mm/1 in lengths
60g/2 oz French onion soup mix
freshly ground black pepper
1 tablespoon sweet paprika
1–1½ cups sour cream
½ cup parsley, finely chopped

1 Heat butter in a large frying pan, add mushrooms and spring onions and sauté for
   approximately 10 minutes. Add onion soup mix, stir through and cook for about
   5 minutes.
2 Mix together pepper, paprika and sour cream and stir into mushroom mixture. Spoon
   mixture into slow cooker and cook on high for approximately 1–1½ hours or on low for
   2–3 hours. Just before serving, stir in chopped parsley. Serve with brown rice.

Serves 4 • Preparation 35 minutes • Cooking 1–3 hours

Argentinean bean and vegetable stew

1 tablespoon olive oil
1 onion, finely diced
2 cloves garlic, crushed
1 red capsicum (bell pepper), diced
1 jalapeño chilli, deseeded and diced
1 teaspoon sweet paprika
400g/14 oz canned diced tomatoes
2 cups vegetable stock
250g/8 oz new potatoes, quartered
250g/8 oz sweet potato, diced
1 carrot, sliced
400g/14 oz canned cannellini beans, rinsed and drained
200g/7 oz Savoy cabbage, shredded
¼ cup fresh coriander (cilantro), chopped
salt and freshly ground black pepper

1 Heat oil in a large frying pan over medium heat. Cook onion, garlic, capsicum (bell pepper) and chilli until soft. Add sweet paprika and cook until aromatic.

2 Transfer contents of frying pan to a slow cooker set on high and add tomatoes and vegetable stock. Stir to combine, then add potato, sweet potato and carrot. Bring to the boil. Reduce heat to low, cover, and simmer for 1½ hours until vegetables are tender.

3 Add beans, cabbage and coriander (cilantro) and season with salt and pepper. Simmer for a further 30 minutes or until cabbage is cooked.

This dish is delicious with crusty bread.

Serves 4 • Preparation 35 minutes • Cooking 1½–2½ hours

Eggplant and tomato casserole

1 medium eggplant, cubed
250g/8 oz tomatoes, sliced
2 cloves garlic, crushed
¼ teaspoon Cayenne pepper or dash of Tabasco
1cm/½ in ginger, grated
1 teaspoon ground coriander
2 bay leaves
1 tablespoon raw sugar
½ cup natural yoghurt

1 Cover eggplant with a handful of salt and allow to stand for approximately an hour. Rinse and drain well.

2 Combine eggplant with all remaining ingredients except yoghurt. Spoon into slow cooker and cook on low for approximately 4 hours. Test to see whether eggplant is cooked.

3 Turn setting to high, stir in the yoghurt and heat through. Remove bay leaves and serve. Each serving may be sprinkled with wholemeal breadcrumbs fried in a little butter, if desired.

Serves 4 • Preparation 90 minutes • Cooking 4 hours

Vegetable curry

2 tablespoons vegetable oil
1kg/2 lb leeks, thinly sliced and washed
500g/1 lb baby carrots, scrubbed and sliced diagonally
4 stalks celery, finely chopped
½ clove garlic, crushed
1 tablespoon curry powder
¾ cup vegetable stock
2 teaspoons cornflour (cornstarch)
salt and freshly ground black pepper
6 spring onions, sliced diagonally

1 Heat the oil in a frying pan and lightly sauté the leeks, carrots and celery. Spoon vegetables into slow cooker. Add garlic and curry powder to frying pan and cook for 1–2 minutes.

2 Blend stock with cornflour (cornstarch), add to frying pan and bring to the boil, stirring constantly. Pour mixture into slow cooker and season. Cook on low for approximately 4 hours or on high for approximately 2–3 hours (test for tenderness after this, as cooking time can very greatly according to the tenderness of the vegetables).

3 When vegetables are cooked, add spring onions. Serve with rice.

Serves 4–6 • Preparation 30 minutes • Cooking 2–4 hours

Moroccan root vegetable curry

1 tablespoon olive oil
1 onion, chopped
1 green chilli, deseeded and chopped
1 clove garlic, finely chopped
25mm/1 in piece ginger, grated
2 tablespoons plain (all-purpose) flour
2 teaspoons ground coriander
2 teaspoons ground cumin
2 teaspoons ground turmeric
1 cup vegetable stock
1 cup tomato purée
750g/1½ lb mixed root vegetables, such as potato, sweet potato,
celeriac and swede (rutabaga), diced
2 carrots, thinly sliced
freshly ground black pepper

1 Heat the oil in a large saucepan. Add the onion, chilli, garlic and ginger and cook, stirring occasionally, for 3 minutes. Stir in the flour, coriander, cumin and turmeric and cook gently, stirring, for 2 minutes to release the flavours.

2 Transfer mixture to a slow cooker and stir in the stock, then add the tomato purée, diced root vegetables and carrots. Season with pepper and mix well. Cook on high for 3¼ hours or until the vegetables are tender. Serve with steamed couscous and garnish with coriander (cilantro).

Serves 4 • Preparation 30 minutes • Cooking 3½ hours

Leeks with beans

250g/8 oz dried black eyed (navy) beans, soaked overnight
1 tablespoon vegetable oil
1 large onion, chopped
2 cloves garlic, crushed
500g/1 lb leeks, sliced and washed
¼ cup parsley, chopped
6 tomatoes, peeled, deseeded and chopped
1 tablespoon raw sugar
1 teaspoon mustard powder
2 bay leaves
½ teaspoon dried marjoram
1 tablespoon tomato paste
¼ cup vegetable stock
salt and freshly ground black pepper

1 Drain the beans well. Heat the oil in a frying pan and sauté the onion and garlic, then add the leeks and sauté until softened. Spoon leek mixture, beans and all remaining ingredients into slow cooker.

2 Cover and cook on low for approximately 8–9 hours or on high for 4–5 hours. Garnish with extra parsley.

Serves 6 • Preparation 25 minutes • Cooking 4–9 hours

baking

Suddenly the old fashioned cooking skills we thought were out of date have become very important and fashionable again! One of these is baking your own bread. There is a certain mystique about bread making and more and more people are turning out their own delicious and fragrant homemade breads. The one deterrent for many people is the time factor. However, by using your slow cooker to gently coax along the proving of the bread, the whole process is speeded up without detriment to the finished loaf. Indeed, you may even use the slow cooker for working the yeast right through to the actual cooking of the bread.

Apple and raisin shorties

500g/1 lb cooking apples, peeled and thinly sliced
¼ cup raw sugar
4 cloves
½ cup raisins
zest of 1 lemon
squeeze of lemon juice

Pastry
150g/5 oz butter
250g/8 oz plain (all-purpose) flour
8 teaspoons wholemeal flour
½ teaspoon baking powder
½ teaspoon cinnamon

1 To make pastry, rub butter into combined flour, baking powder and cinnamon.
   Add a little water and knead very lightly to a manageable dough. Set aside to cool.
2 Place apples in slow cooker with 1 tablespoon water and all other filling ingredients
   and cook for around 3 hours on low or until apples are tender. Test apples from time
   to time. Remove cloves and if mixture is too wet, drain. Allow to cool.
3 Preheat the oven to 200°C/400°F. Roll out the pastry on a floured board and cut out
   10–12 pastry bases and the same numbers of tops. Line small, greased cupcake tins
   with pastry bases, spoon in a little filling, then press tops into place and make a vent
   hole in the crust. Bake for about 45 minutes.
4 Sprinkle shorties with a little icing (confectioner's) sugar and serve either hot with
   cream as a dessert or cold as an afternoon treat.

Makes 10–12 • Preparation 40 minutes • Cooking 3–4 hours

Yoghurt banana bread

60g/2 oz butter
120g/4 oz caster (superfine) sugar
1 egg, lightly beaten
2 large bananas, pulped
250g/8 oz self-raising wholemeal flour
pinch of salt
120g/4 oz walnuts, roughly chopped
3 tablespoons natural yoghurt

1 Cream together the butter and caster (superfine) sugar. Add egg and banana pulp and mix thoroughly.

2 Mix flour and salt together and add walnuts. Add flour mixture and yoghurt alternately to the banana mixture in small quantities, and blend thoroughly.

3 Grease a 12 x 22cm loaf tin, spoon in mixture and cover with lid. Place in slow cooker and cook on high for approximately 2½–3 hours or until a skewer inserted in the banana bread comes out clean. Allow to cool for 10 minutes then turn out onto a wire rack to cool fully.

4 Sprinkle with mixed cinnamon and icing (confectioner's) sugar and serve sliced and spread with butter.

Makes 1 loaf • Preparation 40 minutes • Cooking 3 hours

Cherry and walnut fruit cake

250g/8 oz butter
250g/8 oz brown sugar
5 eggs, beaten to a froth
500g/1 lb sultanas (golden raisins)
170g/6 oz glacé cherries
120g/4 oz walnut pieces
200g/7 oz plain (all-purpose) flour
1 tablespoon milk

1 Cream the butter and sugar in a bowl. Add eggs gradually. Fold in fruit, walnuts and flour, then add milk.

2 Grease a 22cm springform cake tin and line its sides and base with baking paper. Spoon in the cake mixture, cover and place in slow cooker. Cook on high for 4½–5 hours, taking care not to remove either the cooker or the cake tin lid until the last hour of cooking.

Makes 1 cake • Preparation 30 minutes • Cooking 5 hours

Rich berry dessert cake

120g/4 oz butter
¼ cup white sugar
1½ teaspoon vanilla extract
2 eggs, lightly beaten
2 cups plain (all-purpose) flour
2 teaspoons baking powder
salt
1 teaspoon mixed spice
½ cup milk
¾ cup berries of your choice

1 Cream the butter, sugar and vanilla, then fold eggs into mixture.
2 Sift flour, baking powder and salt together and stir in mixed spice. Add spiced flour and milk alternately to the butter mixture, folding in gently and commencing and concluding with the flour. Spoon into a greased and floured 20cm springform cake tin, smooth the surface and arrange berries on top.
3 Cover and place in slow cooker. Cook on high for approximately 3 hours, taking care not to remove either the cooker or the cake tin lid until the last hour of cooking. Sprinkle with cinnamon and icing (confectioner's) sugar and serve hot or cold, with thickened cream.

Serves 8 • Preparation 30 minutes • Cooking 3 hours

Viennese coffee cake

130g/4½ oz butter
¾ cup caster (superfine) sugar
½ teaspoon vanilla extract
3 eggs
1½ cups plain (all-purpose) flour, sifted
1½ teaspoons baking powder
pinch of salt
1 tablespoon milk

Coffee syrup
1 cup strong black coffee
⅓ cup raw sugar
2 tablespoons brandy or whisky

1 Beat the butter until softened, then gradually beat in the sugar and vanilla until mixture is light and fluffy. Add eggs one at a time, beating well after each.

2 Sift together flour, baking powder and salt and fold into butter mixture. Add milk – mixture should have a dropping consistency. Spoon into a greased 20cm springform cake tin, cover, and place tin in slow cooker. Cook on high for about 2–2½ hours, taking care not to remove either the cooker or the cake tin lid until the last 1 hour to 30 minutes of cooking time.

3 Remove tin from slow cooker, allow to cool for about 10 minutes, then turn cake out of tin and allow to cool on a wire rack. When cold, replace in tin.

4 To make the coffee syrup, place the coffee into a saucepan, add sugar and ⅔ cup water and heat until sugar dissolves. Add the brandy or whisky and bring to the boil, stirring occasionally. Boil for 3 minutes. Allow to cool.

5 Pour cold syrup over cake and refrigerate overnight. Serve with cream.

Serves 8 • Preparation 30 minutes • Cooking 2½ hours

Slow cooker health loaf

½ cup unprocessed bran
¾ cup raw sugar
½ cup sultanas (golden raisins)
1 cup raisins
1¼ cups sour milk or buttermilk
1½ cups wholemeal flour
1½ teaspoons baking powder
¼ cup wheatgerm
¼ cup walnuts, chopped

1 Combine bran, sugar, sultanas (golden raisins), raisins and milk and allow to stand for approximately 15 minutes.
2 Mix together the flour, baking powder, wheatgerm and walnuts, then add to the fruit mixture and mix thoroughly. Spoon mixture into a greased 22cm springform cake tin, smooth the surface and cover.
3 Place in slow cooker and cook on high for approximately 3 hours, taking care not to remove either the cooker or the cake tin lid until the last hour of cooking. Remove tin from slow cooker, remove the lid and allow loaf to cool slightly, then turn out onto a wire rack to cool fully.
4 Serve sliced and spread with butter.

Try this loaf sliced and spread with butter and honey or apricot jam.

Makes 1 loaf • Preparation 40 minutes • Cooking 3 hours

Slow cooker country loaf

1 tablespoon compressed yeast
2 teaspoons honey
250g/8 oz plain (all-purpose) flour
120g/4 oz wholemeal flour
2 teaspoons baking powder
1 teaspoon salt
½ cup fine oatmeal
30g/1 oz butter

1 Blend together yeast and honey and pour in 1¼ cups warm water. Sprinkle a little of the flour onto the surface of the liquid and stand bowl over a slow cooker set on low until mixture froths.

2 Mix together all dry ingredients and rub in the butter. Make a well in the centre of the dry ingredients and pour in frothy yeast mixture. Stir with a wooden spoon, then turn out onto a floured board and knead for about 10 minutes. Shape into a round and place back into bowl and set aside on the slow cooker (still set on low) until dough has doubled in size.

3 Punch down risen dough and form into a round. Place in a greased 20cm springform cake tin, cover, and place tin in the slow cooker. Cook on high for about 3–4 hours, then turn loaf out and allow to cool on a wire rack.

Makes 1 loaf • Preparation 30 minutes • Cooking 3–4 hours

Herb bread

1 tablespoon compressed yeast
1 teaspoon white sugar
500g/1 lb plain (all-purpose) flour
1 teaspoon vegetable or garlic salt
2 teaspoons dried mixed herbs
2 teaspoons dried chives, crumbled
2 sprigs parsley, chopped
30g/1 oz butter

1 Crumble the yeast into a bowl, stir in sugar and 1¼ cups lukewarm water until yeast has dissolved. Sprinkle with a little of the flour and stand in a warm spot until mixture froths.

2 Mix together flour, salt and herbs. Rub in the butter, then make a well in the centre of the dry ingredients and pour in frothy yeast mixture. Stir well with a wooden spoon, then turn out onto a floured board and knead for about 5 minutes. Shape into a round, place back into bowl and set aside on a slow cooker set on low until dough has doubled in size.

3 Punch down risen dough and form into a round. Place in a greased 22cm springform cake tin and set aside on the slow cooker again until dough has doubled in size.

4 Cover tin, place in the slow cooker and cook on high for 2–3 hours, taking care not to remove either the cooker or the cake tin lid until the last hour of cooking time. Turn loaf out and allow to cool on a wire rack. Serve dusted with a little extra flour.

Makes 1 loaf • Preparation 40 minutes • Cooking 2–3 hours

Cracked wheat one-rise bread

45g/1½ oz compressed yeast
1 tablespoon treacle (blackstrap molasses)
500g/1 lb wholemeal flour
250g/8 oz plain (all-purpose) flour
¾ cup cracked wheat
1 teaspoon salt

1   In a large bowl, blend together yeast and treacle (blackstrap molasses), then add 2 cups warm water. Mix well, sprinkle a little flour onto surface and set aside in a slow cooker set on low until mixture froths.

2   Mix together all dry ingredients. Pour in frothy yeast mixture and stir with a wooden spoon, then turn out onto a floured board and knead for at least 5 minutes, until mixture is smooth and pliable. Shape into a rough loaf, place in a greased 12 x 22cm loaf tin and set aside on the slow cooker (still set on low) until dough has doubled in size.

3   Preheat the oven to 200°C/400°F. Bake the bread for 10 minutes, then reduce temperature to 190°C/375°F. Continue baking for about another 40 minutes, then test loaf – when cooked, loaf will give a hollow sound when rapped with knuckles. Turn loaf out of tin and allow to cool on a wire rack.

Makes 1 loaf • Preparation 90 minutes • Cooking 2 hours

Half and half loaf

2 tablespoons compressed yeast
2 teaspoons molasses or honey
2⅓ cups warm milk
500g/1 lb plain (all-purpose) flour
500g/1 lb wholemeal flour
1 tablespoon baking powder
1 tablespoon salt
60g/2 oz butter
6 tablespoons sesame seeds
1 egg white

1 Blend together yeast and molasses or honey, then add the milk. Sprinkle a little of the flour on top of the liquid. Stand bowl in a warm spot until mixture froths.

2 Mix together the flours, baking powder and salt. Rub in the butter. Make a well in centre of the dry ingredients and pour in the frothy yeast mixture. Stir well with a wooden spoon, then turn out onto a floured board and knead for about 5 minutes. Shape into a round, place back into bowl and set aside on a slow cooker set on low until dough has doubled in size.

3 Grease two 500g/1 lb bread tins and sprinkle half the sesame seeds around base and sides of tin. Punch down risen dough and form into two rough loaves, then place in tins. Set aside on the slow cooker again until dough has risen to the top of the tins.

4 Preheat the oven to 200°C/400°F. Brush risen loaves with egg white and sprinkle with sesame seeds, then place into oven on middle shelf. Bake for 10 minutes, then reduce temperature to 175°C/350°F and bake for a further 40–45 minutes. Turn loaves out of tins and allow to cool on a wire rack.

Makes 2 loaves • Preparation 90 minutes • Cooking 2 hours

desserts

To many of us, the dessert is the highlight of a meal. It gives the cook the opportunity to show off a little and the guests or family an excuse for a touch of self indulgence. Your slow cooker is a great asset here. Desserts ranging from a sturdy steamed pudding to a delicate apple mousse may be created in your slow cooker and always with a minimum of effort on your part. Start your dessert cooking early in the day, then forget about it until dinnertime. Slow-cooked desserts have a rich, moist taste so you may have to cook a little more for second helpings.

Apricot mousse

250g/8 oz dried apricots
2 floury cooking apples, peeled and thinly sliced
juice and zest of 1 lemon
¼ cup raw sugar
3 egg whites
½ cup thickened cream, whipped

1 Soak dried apricots for approximately 1 hour, then drain well. Place into slow cooker with apples, lemon juice and zest and sugar. Cook on low for 3–4 hours or on high for 2–3 hours, until apricots are soft and apples cooked. Drain fruit, discarding liquid, and purée in a blender or food processor. Chill.

2 Beat egg whites until stiff. Beat the cream in a separate bowl, then fold half the cream into the egg whites. Carefully fold egg white mixture and remaining cream through the fruit purée. Chill. Serve mousse with extra cream and a little grated orange zest.

Serves 4 • Preparation 90 minutes • Cooking 2–4 hours

Ginger custard with choc-ginger sauce

2 large eggs
1¼ cups milk
1 tablespoon sugar
1 tablespoon preserved ginger, finely chopped
½ teaspoon ground ginger
¼ teaspoon ground cinnamon

Choc-ginger sauce
30g/1 oz dark chocolate, grated
2 teaspoons sugar
1 tablespoon ginger wine
⅔ cup evaporated milk
2 teaspoons cornflour (cornstarch)

1 To make the sauce, combine the grated chocolate, sugar, ginger wine and half the milk in a small saucepan. Heat gently until chocolate melts, stirring constantly.

2 Mix the cornflour (cornstarch) into the remaining milk, then add to the chocolate mixture and whisk until sauce boils. Reduce heat and simmer for approximately 3 minutes.

3 To make the custards, beat together eggs, milk and sugar, then stir in chopped ginger. Pour into 2–3 small ovenproof dishes. Sprinkle each dish with a little ginger and cinnamon, then cover with aluminium foil, place in slow cooker and cook for approximately 1½ hours on high or 2–2½ hours on low. Serve custards drizzled with hot choc-ginger sauce.

Serves 2–3 • Preparation 35 minutes • Cooking 1½–2½ hours

Grand Marnier crème caramel

6 tablespoons white sugar
3 eggs
2½ cups milk
2 tablespoons Grand Marnier

1 Melt half the sugar slowly in a heavy saucepan. Do not stir, just allow to melt into toffee.
2 Butter 4 small heatproof crème caramel moulds, then pour the melted sugar quickly into base of dishes and swirl around the sides as high as possible.
3 Beat eggs well and whisk into milk with Grand Marnier and the remaining sugar. Keep whisking until sugar has dissolved, then pour mixture into caramel moulds and cover with foil. Place moulds into slow cooker and pour sufficient cold water around the bases to come halfway up the sides. Cook on low for approximately 3–4 hours.
4 Remove crème caramels from slow cooker and chill thoroughly. Serve either in the moulds or very carefully turned out onto plates, with any caramel left behind spooned over the top.

Serves 4 • Preparation 40 minutes • Cooking 3–4 hours

Butterscotch and apricot parfait

500g/1 lb fresh apricots
1 tablespoon sugar
1 cinnamon stick
pinch of ground nutmeg
1–2 ripe mangoes, peeled and sliced
½ cup thickened cream, whipped
4 sprigs mint

Butterscotch custard
4 egg yolks
400g/14 oz canned evaporated skim milk
1 teaspoon vanilla extract
1 heaped tablespoon dark sugar

1 To make the custard, beat together all the ingredients until sugar has dissolved, then pour into a greased heatproof basin. Cover basin tightly with foil, place in slow cooker, and pour enough water into cooker to come halfway up the sides of the basin. Cook on low for 3–4 hours. Remove basin from slow cooker, loosen around the rim of the basin with a knife and slip custard onto a warmed plate.

2 Wash and stone the apricots, then place them in the slow cooker with sugar, cinnamon stick, nutmeg, and 1 tablespoon water to prevent sticking. Cook on high for at least 2 hours, until tender and almost mushy. Remove cinnamon stick and drain fruit.

3 Set aside 4–6 mango slices for garnish, then layer apricots, butterscotch custard and mangoes in tall parfait glasses until full. Top each glass with a swirl of cream.

Serves 4–6 • Preparation 40 minutes • Cooking 5–6 hours

Ripe fruit compote

6 apricots, halved and stoned
150g/5 oz cherries
6 fresh plums
1 apple, sliced
½ cup sugar
rind of 1 orange
3 cloves

1 Combine all ingredients in the slow cooker and cook on low for 2–3 hours or on high for 1–1½ hours. Remove cloves and orange rind and test for sweetness, adding sugar or honey to taste.

2 Allow to cool, then serve with cream.

This is a marvellous recipe for using up overripe fruit.

Serves 4 • Preparation 10 minutes • Cooking 1–3 hours

Flambé fruit bowl

800g/28 oz canned pears, drained
800g/28 oz canned peach halves, drained
440g/15½ oz canned pineapple slices
12 soft prunes
6 bananas, sliced
12 glacé cherries
⅓ cup orange juice
½ cup juice from canned pineapple
⅓ cup raw sugar
2 tablespoons dark rum
2 cinnamon sticks

1 Layer all fruits except bananas and glacé cherries in the slow cooker. Combine orange and pineapple juice, sugar, half the rum and the cinnamon sticks, then add to slow cooker. Cook on low for 2–3 hours.

2 Remove fruit from slow cooker and place in a heated, shallow ovenproof dish with the bananas and cherries. Discard cinnamon sticks. To serve, heat remaining rum in a small saucepan, set alight and pour quickly over fruit. Serve with cream.

Serves 6–8 • Preparation 15 minutes • Cooking 2–3 hours

Spiced peaches

handful of cloves
600g/21 oz canned peach halves, with juice
1 cinnamon stick
2 tablespoons brandy, orange liqueur or orange juice

1 Press 5 cloves into each peach half and arrange halves in the base of the slow cooker.
2 Combine peach juice and brandy, liqueur or orange juice, add the cinnamon stick and pour mixture over peaches. Cook on low for 2–3 hours or on high for 1–1½ hours. Serve hot or chilled, with cream.

The peaches will keep in the refrigerator for at least a week.

Serves 4 • Preparation 10 minutes • Cooking 1–3 hours

Cherries Grand Marnier

1¼ kg/44 oz canned cherries
rind of 1 orange
2 cinnamon sticks
4 tablespoons Grand Marnier

1 Drain cherries and retain half the syrup. Pour cherries, retained syrup, orange rind and cinnamon sticks into the slow cooker and cook on low for approximately 1 hour. Add half the Grand Marnier and heat through. Remove the cinnamon and orange rind.

2 Serve in individual bowls topped with a scoop of ice cream, a spoonful of the remaining Grand Marnier and a sprinkle of grated chocolate.

Alternatively, for a dinner party, serve the cherries in a large bowl and pour heated flaming Grand Marnier over the cherries at the table.

Serves 8 • Preparation 15 minutes • Cooking 1 hour

Cherry orchard bowl

500g/1 lb cherries
1½ cups rosé wine
3 tablespoons sugar
1 cinnamon stick
2 tablespoons brandy or Grand Marnier
zest of 1 orange, grated
250g/8 oz strawberries

1 Place cherries in slow cooker, pour over the rosé and add the sugar, cinnamon stick and liqueur. Cover tightly and cook for approximately 2 hours on low.

2 Add the orange zest and strawberries and chill well. Serve with cream.

Serves 6–8 • Preparation 10 minutes • Cooking 2 hours

Bananas in rum and honey syrup

6 firm bananas, peeled
2 tablespoons dark rum
1 tablespoon honey
2 tablespoons orange juice
juice of ½ lemon
½ teaspoon ground cinnamon

1 Arrange bananas in base of slow cooker. Combine rum, honey, juices and cinnamon and spoon over and around bananas. Cook on high for approximately ½–¾ hour or on low for approximately 1 hour, until bananas are just tender and syrup is heated through.
2 Serve bananas with scoops of ice cream, with syrup spooned over.

Serves 4–6 • Preparation 15 minutes • Cooking 30–60 minutes

Dundee marmalade pudding

2 cups milk
120g/4 oz fresh, fine breadcrumbs
3 eggs, separated
60g/2 oz caster (superfine) sugar
2 tablespoons dark marmalade

1 Bring milk to the boil and pour over breadcrumbs. Allow to cool.
2 Beat the egg yolks with the sugar, then add the marmalade. Stir into the cold bread and milk mixture. Beat the egg whites until stiff and fold in.
3 Grease a pudding basin and lightly spoon in the pudding mixture. Cover basin tightly with foil and tie with kitchen string, forming a loop at the top so that the basin may be easily removed from the slow cooker. Place basin into cooker, pour over boiling water and cook on high for about 3 hours.
4 Remove basin, carefully turn out pudding and serve with hot custard.

Serves 4–6 • Preparation 25 minutes • Cooking 3 hours

Lemon sago pudding

1 cup uncooked sago
1 large egg
1 cup milk
1–2 tablespoons raw sugar
1 teaspoon vanilla extract
½ teaspoon ground nutmeg
zest of 1 lemon, grated

1 Bring 1 cup water to a fast boil and pour in the sago. Cook at a quick simmer, stirring often, until sago is translucent (about 15 minutes). If the water is absorbed before the sago is cooked, add a little more. When done, pour the sago into a bowl and allow to cool.

2 Beat together the egg, milk and sugar in a bowl, then add remaining ingredients and sago. Pour mixture into a lightly greased dish, sprinkle with extra nutmeg and cover with a lid or foil.

3 Place dish in the slow cooker, and carefully pour enough hot water around the dish to come three-quarters of the way up its sides. Cook on high for 2 hours or on low for 3 hours, then serve hot or cold with stewed fruit and whipped cream.

Serves 4 • Preparation 40 minutes • Cooking 2–3 hours

Creamy rice pudding

zest of 1 orange, grated
2½ cups cooked rice
1 cup evaporated milk or 1 cup ordinary milk plus 1 beaten egg
⅔ cup raw sugar
60g/2 oz butter, softened
½ teaspoon vanilla extract
½ teaspoon ground cinnamon or nutmeg
⅓ cup sultanas (golden raisins)

1 Reserve a little orange zest to garnish, then mix the rice with all other ingredients. Lightly grease the slow cooker interior and spoon in pudding mixture.

2 Cook on high for approximately 1–2 hours or on low for 4–6 hours. Stir occasionally during first hour of cooking. Serve with a little cream and a pinch of grated orange zest.

Serves 6 • Preparation 30 minutes • Cooking 1–6 hours

Caramel rice and apricot pudding

1 cup evaporated milk
1 teaspoon vanilla extract
⅔ cup soft brown sugar
2½ cups rice, cooked but still slightly firm
60g/2 oz butter, melted
½ teaspoon mixed spice
½ cup canned apricots, drained

1 Beat together evaporated milk, vanilla and sugar. Combine with remaining ingredients, pour mixture into a greased ovenproof dish and cover with foil

2 Place dish in slow cooker and cook on high for 1½–2 hours or on low for 4–6 hours. Stir occasionally during the first 30 minutes or so of cooking.

This dish is best served hot.

Serves 6 • Preparation 15 minutes • Cooking 1½–6 hours

Baked bread and butter pudding

4 thin slices stale brown or white bread, buttered
½ cup mixed sultanas (golden raisins) and currants
3 tablespoons raw sugar
½ teaspoon grated nutmeg or cinnamon
2 eggs
2½ cups milk
1 teaspoon vanilla extract
zest of ½ orange, grated

1 Remove crusts from bread and cut into thick fingers. Grease an ovenproof dish and arrange bread in layers, buttered-side up. Sprinkle layers with dried fruit, sugar and spice.

2 Beat together eggs, milk and vanilla and stir in orange zest. Pour mixture over layered bread and allow to stand for approximately 30 minutes. Cover dish with lid or foil.

3 Pour 1 cup hot water into the slow cooker, then insert the pudding dish and cook on high for 3–4 hours.

Serves 6 • Preparation 45 minutes • Cooking 3–4 hours

Country currant pie

340g/12 oz currants
½ cup sugar
1 tablespoon cornflour (cornstarch)
juice and zest of 1 lemon

Pastry
150g/5 oz butter
1½ cups plain (all-purpose) flour
1½ teaspoons baking powder

1 To make the pastry, place the butter in a large bowl, pour in 2 tablespoons boiling water and mash the butter slightly. Sift in the flour and baking powder and stir until mixture comes together, adding a little more flour if necessary until pastry is smooth and manageable. Allow to stand until firm and easy to handle.

2 Combine currants, sugar, cornflour (cornstarch) and lemon juice and zest with ½ cup water in the slow cooker. Cook for around 1 hour on high (this filling must be cooked on high to ensure the cornflour (cornstarch) cells burst and thicken it). Allow to cool.

3 Preheat the oven to 200°C/400°F. Reserve one-third of the pastry for the pie crust and roll out the remainder roughly on a floured board. Grease a 20cm/8 in pie dish and press pastry into the base and sides, then spoon in the currant filling.

4 Roll the reserved pastry out between two sheets of baking paper. Peel off one sheet of the paper, invert the pastry onto the pie, then remove the remaining sheet. Pinch the pie edges together, trim any excess, and use the pastry scraps to create a decoration for the crust. Sprinkle with caster (superfine) sugar and bake for approximately 45–50 minutes. Serve with cream.

Serves 6–8 • Preparation 40 minutes • Cooking 1–2 hours

Orange-wheel steamed pudding

2 oranges, peeled and thickly sliced, plus zest of 1 orange
90g/3 oz butter
½ cup raw sugar
1½ cups self-raising flour
salt
½ cup milk
1 egg, beaten
2 tablespoons golden (cane) syrup or honey

1 Grease a medium-sized pudding basin and arrange orange slices around the base and sides.
2 Cream together butter and sugar until light and fluffy. Stir in flour and salt to taste alternately with milk and egg, then beat until smooth. Stir in grated orange zest.
3 Warm golden (cane) syrup or honey and spoon over the base and sides of the orange-lined basin. Spoon in pudding mixture, cover basin tightly with foil and tie with string, forming a loop at the top so that the basin may be easily removed from the slow cooker.
4 Place basin in slow cooker. Boil 2–4 cups water and pour into base of cooker, then cook on high for approximately 5 hours. Carefully remove the pudding basin and turn pudding out. Slice the pudding and serve with a little extra warmed golden (cane) syrup or honey spooned over each slice, topped with a dab of cream.

Serves 6–8 • Preparation 75 minutes • Cooking 5 hours

Fruity-favourite steamed pudding

90g/3 oz butter
1 cups caster (superfine) sugar
2 cups plain (all-purpose) flour
1½ teaspoons baking powder
½ teaspoon mixed spice
½ teaspoon baking soda
salt
½ cup milk
1 egg
1 tablespoon raisins
1 tablespoon sultanas (golden raisins)
1 tablespoon dried dates, chopped
1 tablespoon dried apricots, chopped
1 tablespoon walnuts, chopped

1 Grease a medium-sized pudding basin with a little of the butter. Cream the remainder with caster (superfine) sugar in a separate basin, until light and soft.

2 Stir flour and baking powder together with mixed spice, baking soda and salt to taste. Beat milk and egg together. Stir small quantities of sifted flour and beaten milk alternately into creamed butter mixture. Fold together lightly.

3 Stir in dried fruits and walnuts, and spoon mixture into basin. Cover tightly with foil and tie with kitchen string, forming a loop at the top so that the basin may be easily removed from the slow cooker.

4 Place basin in slow cooker and pour enough boiling water around the base to come halfway up the sides. Cook on high for approximately 5 hours. Turn out pudding onto heated serving platter and serve with hot custard.

Serves 6–8 • Preparation 45 minutes • Cooking 5 hours